What Itching Ears Don't Want to Hear

What Itching Ears Don't Want to Hear

A Revelation of Jesus Christ for the End Time Generation

ANDREW M. DENNY

iUniverse, Inc.
Bloomington

WHAT ITCHING EARS DON'T WANT TO HEAR
A Revelation of Jesus Christ for the End Time Generation

iUniverse books may be ordered through booksellers or by contacting:

iUniverse
1663 Liberty Drive
Bloomington, IN 47403
www.iuniverse.com
1-800-Authors (1-800-288-4677)

ISBN: 978-1-4697-7932-4 (sc)
ISBN: 978-1-4697-7933-1 (ebk)

Printed in the United States of America

iUniverse rev. date: 02/25/2012

Contents

Introduction... ix

Chapter 1   What Itching Ears Must First Realize................. 1

Chapter 2   What Itching Ears Tend To Ignore 19

Chapter 3   Salvation Aforetime 43

Chapter 4   Itching Ears' Preferred Tradition 82

Chapter 5   Turning Unto Fables 116

Chapter 6   The Powers That Tickled Our Ears 152

Chapter 7   What Itching Ears Must Conclude................. 178

Overview

As Christians we are expected to be able to tell people *why* we believe *what* we believe (I Peter 3:15). Additionally, we are to do so by correctly explaining the Bible from the context in which it was written (II Timothy 2:15). This means that, no matter what denomination we may be a part of, we as claimed Christians during these last days need to lay aside our personal biases in order to further understand how the *apostles* perceived the Gospel.

Not to imply that any church denomination is "wrong" for any particular view; maybe just incomplete for not fully comprehending the teachings of the Lord Jesus Christ to the measure of the men who actually heard Him.

Some may call this work just a "theory," but what this book offers is a *prospect* of what the apostles essentially gathered from the man Jesus, along with the principles He instituted—apart from the typical view of today's modernized audience, that is. As we take a look into the development of the early church from a different angle we will examine certain words and actions taken by the apostles which commonly go unnoticed.

In other words, we should be able to detect which New Testament doctrines have been swept under the rug by modern tradition. By the end of this endeavor you alone must determine whether this book should be classified as *fact* or *fiction*. You alone must decide whether or not you will apply these things.

> You alone must . . .
> . . . work out your own salvation with fear and trembling.
> —Philippians 2:12

For the time will come when they will not endure sound doctrine; but after their own lusts shall they heap to themselves teachers, having itching ears; And they shall turn away their ears from the truth, and shall be turned unto fables.

—II Timothy 4:3-4

Introduction

My son, despiseth not the chastening of the LORD; neither be weary of his correction: For whom the LORD loveth he correcteth;

—Proverbs 3:11-12

As a member of a church that urges the encouragement of one another I do not believe it is wise to strike up a conversation by harshly pointing out one's errors or bluntly telling someone they are "wrong" for something they may or may not believe. Understanding this reality first-hand (through experience), *correction* can be very tricky whereas it tends to raise feelings of defensiveness to the person on the receiving end. It can either *en*courage or *dis*courage others. Yet a major factor involved, which may determine the final outcome, is the initial *approach* of the one correcting. In fact, our words may very easily be misunderstood—even twisted—if we are not wise in our approach. For that reason I would like to begin by commending you rather—or at least those of you who can humbly admit when you *are* wrong. (No, this isn't reverse psychology.)

Here's why:

Today with all the various types of Christian churches abroad it's no secret that there are variances in doctrine among the Christian faith. Even though the Bible speaks against division (Luke 11:17, I Cor 1:10) we as Christians have, throughout the course of time, failed to uphold the principle of *unity* by forming countless church denominations and endorsing a wide range of doctrines. While this issue is one that the majority will continue to ignore rather than acknowledge, the reality will never cease to exist.

Division, being one of the more visible motes within the eye of Christianity, consequently brings to light the most visible mote within us; that is, hypocrisy. For believing in "one body" and being of "one mind" the Christian faith more or less publicizes its hypocrisy simply because of denominationalism. Even though you and I may not personally be responsible for the different forms of Christianity, we as the "body of Christ"—or at least those of us who claim to be—must be willing to humbly admit (as a whole) the error of our ways. Furthermore, while the problem of division goes against our guidelines as a church it has an effect on our individual perception of Christianity as well. It shapes—or at least plays a part in shaping—our own personal views of what "Truth" is.

Here's how:

If we hold fast to a specific doctrine or belief then we must be able to tell people WHY we believe WHAT we believe. Not only are we expected by others to defend our faith, ultimately God expects the same as well. Our instructions as Christians are to *always be ready to give an answer to everyone about our hope in Christ* (I Peter 3:15). Even though this instruction applies to each and every person who claims to be a Christian—no matter what his or her denominational code may be—it is more common to hear people defend his or her faith by using simple statements such as:

"That's just your interpretation of Scripture; my opinion is a little different."

"Let's just 'agree to disagree' about our views of the Bible."

Unfortunately the problem with this mindset in some cases (depending on the topic) is that it opposes our guidelines as Christians. Notice the following impartation:

> Now I beseech you, brethren, by the name of our Lord Jesus Christ, that ye all speak the same thing, and that there be no divisions among you; but that ye be perfectly joined together in the same mind and in the same judgment.
>
> —I Corinthians 1:10

Because the Bible speaks against different opinions of the Gospel and divisions among Christianity, basically, *agreeing-to-disagree* is a sin. (Don't jump to any conclusions yet.) Most likely the majority of Christians already understand that we all have our own personal convictions and that one person's commitment to God may be different than the next. One person for instance may be able to listen to a certain type of music with absolutely *no* conviction while another may feel *deeply* convicted about it. Also, this person may be able to read a certain Biblical passage and be enlightened while the other person may gain nothing from the same Scripture until years later. Nonetheless, when it comes to the *absolute principles* of Christianity we cannot afford to have interpretational variances when discussing the Gospel. As the passage above states, we must *"speak the same thing."* Furthermore, the Apostle Paul even assures us that we can understand the Gospel from what is plainly written in Scripture:

> For we write none other things unto you, than what ye read or acknowledge;
>
> —II Corinthians 1:13

Therefore I will be addressing certain matters that are commonly *disputed* by some, *ignored* by others, *veiled* from the eyes of many, and yet are *plainly* written in black and white throughout both the Bible and secular history. I believe this book suggests to its readers three contemplative questions:

➢ How humble are you (Psalm 69:32)?
➢ How hungry are you (Jeremiah 29:13)?
➢ Are you "testing the spirits" (I John 4:1)?

Please refer back to the previous questions in the event of reading something that challenges or disagrees with your current views. (Some ideas may be difficult to take hold of.) Nonetheless—and to get down to the point of discussion—much of this book was written in order to pin-point exactly who or what the Apostle Peter was referring to in his warning to the saints abroad. The Network:

❖ But there were false prophets also among the people, <u>even as there shall be false teachers among you, who privily shall bring damnable heresies</u>, even denying the Lord that bought them, and bring upon themselves swift destruction.

           —II Peter 2:1

First and foremost we must accept that there are false teachers among the Christian faith. Don't worry. This book does not specifically point out the names of any particular individual of the modern-day churches; it addresses and challenges Christianity as a whole in order to make the body of Christ stronger and more aware. Specifically, one matter of concern is that there are teachers *in general* among the Christian faith who are currently fulfilling Peter's warning by preaching that certain models throughout the Bible do not pertain to our salvation; that is, since we are "covered by grace."

Let there be no confusion; we *are* saved by grace. Yet we must realize that we cannot neglect the commands of God under the *assumption* that God's grace will still cover us. And if this is what we believe then we are "taking God's grace in vain" (II Cor 6:1). The Bible even talks about how men have perverted (or changed) the grace of God into a license for immorality (Jude 1:4). Notice the following passage as Christ asks:

> *And why call ye me, Lord, Lord, and do not the things which I say?*
>
> —Luke 6:46

Should we actually consider ourselves *worthy* to call Him "Lord" if we do not make a continual effort to obey His commands? Even though the Bible plainly teaches that even the *righteous* will barely be saved (II Peter 4:18) it seems as if modern society admits *everybody* into Heaven (especially during funeral ceremonies). Although, if we truly have the desire to receive God's grace—if we want to be "saved"—then we must understand that we are required to obey the commands of God to the best of our ability (II Thess 1:8).

I understand we're all human and we're going to make mistakes from time to time, but the Bible states that obeying God's commands is how we come to know Him (I John 2:3), how we show God that we love Him (I John 5:3), how we can be confident of our salvation (I John 3:24), and how we fulfill our purpose in life (Eccl 12:13). Basically, from our perspective obeying God's commands is the point of our existence.

Now, as far as these "teachers" I'm referring to, not every false teacher will know that he *is* one. As a matter of fact, many false teachers are unaware of the confusion they've caused. Jesus tells us that, often times they truly believe they are in the will of God (John 16:2), doing a service unto Him. Still, the Bible says *there is a way that seems right unto a man, but the end thereof are the ways of death* (Prov 16:25). These false teachers, who don't want to offend anyone, will tell people what their itching ears want to hear in order to draw large numbers and gratify *congregations*, which brings us to the actual root of the problem. We as a congregation mustn't conclude that the teachers are to blame when WE are the ones who don't want messages that convict us. Observe the Network once again:

❖ For the time will come when they will not endure sound doctrine; but after their own lusts <u>shall they heap to themselves teachers</u>, having itching ears; And they shall turn away their ears from the truth, and shall be turned unto fables.

—II Timothy 4:3

Many of us would rather be told we are doing *enough* for God than to be told we need to put forth a continual effort to please Him. We crave sermons about *peace* and *prosperity* rather than confrontational messages on subjects such as *hypocrisy* or *humility*. We desire preachers who apply the sugar-coated phrase "Bad Habits" instead of those who exercise the word "SIN." And instead of exploring the Word of God to find out Christian truths ourselves we would rather listen to teachers who ensure us that "grace" is the only thing we need in order to be saved. Nonetheless, what the churches of today must realize is that Christianity did not succeed because the Gospel was a *peaceful* message which the world *wanted* to hear. Christian truths have caused more controversies over the past two thousand years than any area under discussion. The world's attitude toward "Truth" is the key factor in what the following verse affirms:

> *Think not that I am come to send peace on earth: I came not to send peace, but a sword.*
>
> —Matthew 10:34

If the Message of Salvation was for the purpose of offering peace and comfort among *people*—more specifically, if the Gospel was meant to gratify *mankind*—then we would never be challenged to do anything for God, whereas He would have simply allowed us to live however we please, never to reap the eternal consequences.

Still, this is only a *fraction* of the premise; the *tip* of the iceberg. The passage above expresses more than just the conflict between Christianity and the secular mainstream; it portrays the spiritual struggle within the individual man of God. When we are confronted with ideas that challenge us spiritually—when we hear the powerful Word of God nudging us away from our complacency—we tend to feel uneasy. This feeling of discomfort is a spiritual reaction within the midst of our body and mind. It is the very grounds for which Paul wrote to Timothy warning him of future generations having itching ears. It's called *Conviction,* and it wages war between the forces of Good and evil. The reaction of conviction only confirms that the physical world, which we *can* see, intertwines and exists within the spirit realm, which we *cannot* see. The author of the book of Hebrews describes this reaction precisely:

> For the word of God is quick, and powerful, and sharper than any twoedged sword, <u>piercing even to the dividing asunder of soul and spirit, and of the joints and marrow, and is a discerner of the thoughts and intents of the heart.</u>
>
> —Hebrews 4:12

Conviction is more or less the reason why Christianity has caused more controversy in the world than any secular religion; it only occurs when Truth is affirmed. When a person feels that two-edged sword he will not be able to obtain peace until he deals with the will of God. There must be an initial response when we hear the powerful Word of God. A perfect example of this can be found in the Book of Acts during the establishment of the church, which occurred just days following Christ's ascension. Men of all regions were dwelling in Jerusalem on that day as Simon-Peter proclaimed the Gospel Message to the world for the first time. As for those who received the Word of God (notice the reaction):

> Now when they heard this, they were pricked in their heart, . . .
>
> —Acts 2:37

Truth stings! When the Word of God is affirmed it's not something that is necessarily *easy* to receive; yet the results—according to *our* response—can be massive. Notice the outcome in this scenario once they considered the facts:

> Then they that gladly received his word were baptized: and <u>the same day there were added unto them about three thousand souls</u>. And they continued steadfastly in the apostles' doctrine, . . .
>
> —Acts 2:41-42

Three thousand souls were added to the Christian faith the same day! Even though many teachers today refuse to convey messages of conviction because they *"don't want to offend anyone"* or *"make anybody feel uncomfortable,"* the truth is that it is according to our response to conviction that makes a difference in our spiritual journey. And while it is our *initial* response that activates our salvation (once we begin to hear the voice of the Lord for the first time), it is our *continual* response that preserves us for the rest of our lives.

Our spiritual awakening comes through obeying principles such as confession, repentance, and baptism, etc; however, it is our faithfulness that determines our eternal reward, whereas we are judged according to *everything* we do here on earth (Rom 2:6-7, Rev 20:13). As a matter of fact *continuance* is one of the chief principles of the Christian faith which we will be discussing. And even though many "Christians" would rather continue feeding our itching ears with sermons guaranteeing us that we've *already* done enough for God—a.k.a. the pat-on-the-back message—my fearful responsibility to God is to convict your soul by offering you . . .

"What Itching Ears Don't Want To Hear!"

1

What Itching Ears Must First Realize

. . . let every man be swift to hear, slow to speak, . . .
—James 1:19

First, let's all just try to avoid forming any opinions until we've read every portion of this book (including the intro). The passage above holds a powerful principle in that one cannot make reasonable judgments without first considering *all* of the facts; otherwise his determination would be based upon assumption. The purpose here is to provide you with *further* insight of what is written in the Bible rather than revisiting those common themes which we are currently familiar with. Furthermore, some of the strongest material is offered in the conclusion. The overall goal is to bring together the true worshipers—no matter what his or her denominational background—in order that everyone may be of the same mind and judgment just as the Bible commands (I Cor 1:10). My intention isn't necessarily to cause division among a particular church body; it is to distinguish the willing from the unwilling.

The Lord may call us out from that which we are accustomed to in order for us to advance spiritually; no matter what our current circumstance, denomination, or religion may be. The disciple Nathaniel (Bartholomew), for instance, was a true Israelite who served the Lord in all sincerity and whose relationship with God was evident. God, however, though He was pleased with Nathaniel's devotion, desired that he "shift gears" in order to take his spiritual journey to the next level (John 1:47-51). Likewise—though Nathaniel's story may be a little more complex than others whereas his conversion involved physical interaction with the Messiah while He was here in the flesh—my desire is to assist you in taking your walk with God above and beyond the norm.

Be Aware: Your flesh will work against you on this endeavor. What I mean is that, we as humans are more likely to look for error with things that challenge us rather than considering everything first. And since one of the most common desires of the flesh is to *reason* with logic, there may be some of you who will find yourselves looking for excuses as to why these things may not apply to you. Although if it is written in the Bible, it applies to You! If Jesus said it, it applies to You! And if the apostles taught it, it applies to You! Don't worry, because when I say, "You," . . . I mean Me too; myself included. So please do not take the "You's" too personally or be offended. If anything, be convicted. I say this because some of you may have a hard time accepting this challenge—or realizing that *you* personally are accountable to certain concepts or models throughout the Bible. That being the case, I will just go ahead and offer two of the most common reasons you may feel this way:

➤ Fear that you may be "wrong" because you have not already seen or understood some of the things this book offers. (Don't worry; nobody is "wrong" simply because he or she may be at a different level spiritually than someone else).
➤ Fear of what your peers may think of you if you should choose to accept this challenge (just as the disciples felt I'm sure).

Now, I'm guessing that many of you—from what you have already read—may have the impression that this is one of those books which says, *"do 'this or that' or you're going to hell."* But seriously, what else would you expect in a book which holds the title *What Itching Ears DON'T Want To Hear?*

Don't jump to any conclusions yet. Even though we may be discussing a few topics that directly affect our salvation the overall purpose is for everyone to mature spiritually. The main thing to understand is that *anything* we do sacrificially for God—any act of obedience—plays a part in our salvation. As I mentioned in the introduction, we are judged by *everything* we choose to do here on earth (Rom 2:6-7, Rev 20:13); therefore, if we humbly take steps toward God then not only will He respond, but ultimately our relationship with Him will become more intimate (James 4:8).

As I previously stated, *anyone* who claims to be a Christian—no matter what his or her denomination—must be in agreement on certain matters. Therefore, every model presented throughout this book will be supported by Scripture in order to affirm exactly what the early church believed. Occasionally you may notice a manner of sternness in the commentary; however, we must remember what the Apostle Paul instructed Titus:

> Wherefore rebuke them sharply, that they may be sound in the faith;
>
> —Titus 1:13

And because it's God's will for everyone to be *"sound in the faith,"* I wish to relay these principles using the same methods the apostles used. Some of you may feel that I am specifically pointing out your error or that my goal is to play the "Who's right or wrong" game. However, that is not my intention. But if you do feel that way . . . it could possibly be conviction. Again, my goal is *not* to tickle your ears; it is to challenge you to become a stronger Christian. That is why I will be presenting a considerable amount of Scripture—for sound teaching, to convict your soul, to correct any misconceptions, and to guide you in holiness:

> All scripture is given by inspiration of God, and is profitable for doctrine, for reproof, for correction, for instruction in righteousness: That the man of God may be perfect, thoroughly furnished unto all good works.
>
> —II Timothy 3:16-17

If something offered throughout this book *does* happen to be a matter of salvation there will be solid Scriptural validation.

Above all there is something that everyone must first be aware of—something which most Christians more than likely understand already: God's judgment is not determined by whether or not we *agree* with His plan of salvation; we must first *accept* it as the truth and subsequently *obey* it. This applies to ALL. God does not show partiality to one type of person over another:

> . . . God is no respecter of persons:
>
> —Acts 10:34

If you find that you disagree with a certain concept in this book, just read on as you may receive your answer in due course. Remember, everyone is required to observe and confirm whether a teaching is from God or the enemy before jumping to any conclusions:

> Beloved, believe not every spirit, but try the spirits whether they are of God: because many false prophets are gone out into the world.
>
> —I John 4:1

We are to be very cautious of certain teachings; however, we are also to consider whether or not WE may be the ones who are in error. We cannot just accept any man's teaching as Truth, whether it is from a pastor, a teacher, or even the Pope himself (especially the Pope) before comparing everything with both biblical and secular history. Once again, this includes ME. Don't listen to me if I cannot back everything up by the Word of God. (Don't worry; this book does not contain any wacky, cultic philosophies.) What this is about is revealing some of the principles in which the *apostles* stood so firm. Still, you may be wondering why I would recommend everyone to be cautious of what I have to offer if this work is something I am trying to enlighten others with. Well, it's because every person is to submit to the Word of God alone, and again, we are to either *confirm* or *reprove* a teaching by comparing it to Scripture. Not only that, we are to do so by correctly explaining the Word of God as well:

> Study to shew thyself approved unto God, . . . rightly
> dividing the word of truth.
>
> —II Timothy 2:15

Remember, I previously mentioned in the summary that, *"You alone must determine whether this book should be classified as Fact or Fiction."* Only you have the ability to decide whether or not you will apply this challenge to your personal walk with God. Therefore, before we go any further I would like to propose a system (in which many will probably end up concluding as "sheer theory"). You may have noticed this system in the intro. Throughout much of this book I'll be attempting to unveil exactly how the Bible works—and *has* worked—as a *Network* in the world around us. Before each composition you should see the ❖ icon. This will let you know that I am attempting to unveil a deep revelation or fulfillment of prophecy. For example—hold on because this is deep—there's something that we must all understand:

❖ The Network:

> For <u>a nation is come up upon my land</u>, strong, and
> without number, whose teeth are the teeth of a lion,
> and he hath the cheek teeth of a great lion. <u>He hath laid
> my vine waste</u>, and barked my fig tree: he hath made
> it clean bare, and cast it away; the branches thereof are
> made white.
>
> —Joel 1:6-7

While the passage above may be confusing to some it is very relevant to the teachings this book offers. And while there is much more to this prophecy (as you will see by reading Chapter 6) I will just sum up what it applies to. This passage (written somewhere between 800 B.C. & 400 B.C.) predicts how the nation of Rome destroyed the New Testament church in which Jesus established through the apostles. If you didn't already know, it was because of the Roman government that many truths about God remained hidden for many centuries. In a nutshell, Rome took over the Christian faith by altering (contaminating) many of the doctrines in which the Lord pre-mandated through the apostles. This was only a few short centuries after the original apostles' ministry had come to an end. But how does this apply to you and me? Well, notice the following prophecy:

> And <u>I will restore to you the years that the locust hath eaten</u>, . . . And ye shall eat in plenty, and be satisfied, and praise the name of the LORD your God, . . . And it shall come to pass afterward, that I will pour out my spirit upon all flesh; and your sons and your daughters shall prophesy, . . . <u>in those days will I pour out my spirit</u>.
> —Joel 2:25-29

Just to sum everything up; here is a brief, brief overview of what was predicted to happen over the past 2,000 years:

➤ The Bible tells us that God established a church through the apostles. (The New Testament is the historical account of this church being established.)

➤ Prophecy informs us that, for a time, Truth would be taken away (hidden) from the world. Many of these "truths" that would be hidden can be summed up by knowing the difference between an *absolute principle* of Christianity and a *man-made tradition* or *doctrine.* (Joel 1:6-7, etc)

➤ Prophecy also informs us that truth (sound doctrine) would be restored (revealed) in the last days; that there would be a remnant of people who would receive revelation as to what was first presented by the Lord and confirmed by the apostles. (Joel 2:25-29, etc)

Basically, even though there are thousands of organizations under the Christian name—as Jesus predicted (Matthew 24:5)—the Bible STILL says there is only one true church body, only one true belief system, and only one hope of being saved:

There is <u>one body</u>, and one Spirit, even as ye are called
in <u>one hope of your calling</u>; One Lord, <u>one faith</u>, one
baptism, One God and Father of all, who is above all,
and through all, and in you all.

—Ephesians 4:4-6

Before we continue let's get something straight: what church
denomination you attend does not define whether you are a part
of the one true body of Christ. The one true church of God cannot
be classified as a "denomination." What defines God's church is:
understanding, believing, and continuing in the same doctrine as the
apostles; that is to say, the doctrine in which Jesus Christ entrusted to
them before Rome's influential destruction. Just like the Christians
of the early apostolic era, we too must continue in the faith:

And they continued steadfastly in the apostles' doctrine . . .

—Acts 2:42

---

†

Now, I've heard some wacky theories in my days as to which church
is the one true church of God. But just for a moment let's discuss
a few of the possibilities. I remember hearing a theory suggesting
that, *"since humans are identified by NAMES then the one true church
will be identified the same way. Therefore, the one true church is none
other than the Church of Christ."* Well . . . Nice try. But again, it does
not depend on the denomination a person attends that determines
whether he is a part of the one true body of Christ. A person could
attend *any* church denomination, and it would still depend on what
he or she believes and applies to themselves. Remember, we are
judged individually (Rom 2:5-7); not as a group.

Furthermore—referring to the Church-of-Christ theory—Christ
is more of a Messianic title than an actual name. Not to discredit
or imply bigotry toward the Church of Christ (I personally know
many wonderful *believers* from this organization), but if this man's
theory were true—if it's all in the name of a church sect—then we

would be forced to say the one true church of God is the *Church of JESUS Christ of Latter Day Saints* (Mormonism), whereas it holds the actual name of the Lord (and we should all know that's not true). Remember, we are to *"test the spirits to see whether they are from God"* (I John 4:1). And when testing the spirit of the Mormon belief we should first remember what Jesus predicted:

> *For many shall come in my name, . . . And many false prophets shall rise, and shall deceive many. For there shall arise false Christs, . . . insomuch that, if it were possible, they shall deceive the very elect.*
> —Matthew 24:5, 11, 24

If you don't know the origin of the Mormon faith, allow me to briefly summarize. Once upon a time, a man named Joseph Smith claimed that an ANGEL of the Lord visited him and gave him a message to share with the world. Thusly—aside from several other anti-scriptural doctrines—Mormonism was born. However, what Mr. Smith failed to realize beforehand is what the Bible forewarned the saints of the true church of God.

❖ The Network:

> But though we, <u>or an angel from heaven</u>, preach any other gospel unto you than that which we have preached unto you, let him be accursed.
> —Galatians 1:8

In effect, whether Smith's claim *was* or was *not* true, the passage above—being the authoritative Word of God—would rule out the angel's message to Mr. Smith. But still, just in case Mr. Smith's claim *was* true—if he really did speak with an angel—then he should have been on his guard . . .

> . . . for Satan himself is transformed into an angel of light.
> —II Corinthians 11:14

Now, since the angel has been ruled out, what about Mr. Smith himself? Should anyone have ever listened to him in the first place? Well, according to the Bible . . .

> If there come any unto you, and bring not this doctrine, receive him not into your house, neither bid him God speed: For he that biddeth him God speed is partaker of his evil deeds.
>
> —II John 10-11

And that disqualifies Mr. Smith. Furthermore—and in conclusion of the matter—the cover of *The Book of Mormon* even states that it is *"ANOTHER Testament of Jesus Christ,"* which also goes against the previous passage in Galatians. Case closed!

One thing we must acknowledge about the devil is this: the cleverest way Satan has devised world religions in the past is by using the Christian faith as the foundation; blending the message of Christ with man-made doctrines. I do not wish to give the devil glory for his tactics; however, we all need to be aware of what he is permitted to do here on earth. Overall we must understand that there are some organizations which can help lead us to Truth, and there are some that could lead us toward destruction. Some organizations are allied with the one true church of God, and some are deceivers and antichrists. Furthermore, why we need to guard ourselves so intently is because many of these deceivers come from *within* the church (I John 2:18-19); they will *appear* to be "Christian." The most sobering thing to realize is that not everyone who claims to be a part of the body of Christ will actually make it to Heaven. Observe the following words of Christ:

> *Not every one that saith unto me, Lord, Lord, shall enter into the kingdom of heaven; . . . Many will say to me in that day, Lord, Lord, have we not prophesied in thy name? and in thy name have cast out devils? and in thy name done many wonderful works? And then will I profess unto them, I never knew you: depart from me, ye that work iniquity.*
>
> —Matthew 7:21-23

Ask yourself: Do these described in the passage above sound like lost sinners who don't know God? Absolutely not! This verse depicts those who claim to be Christians, who have done many works for God, assuming they have done enough to make it to Heaven. Yet it gets even more sobering than this. While the previous passage applies to those who are face to face with Jesus after this life (Judgment Day), the following verse describes those who presently dwell here on earth; who still have the choice of whether or not they will seek God further. Perhaps both passages are referring to the same people. Notice the similarity; notice the response.

> Having a form of godliness, but denying the power thereof: from such turn away.
> —II Timothy 3:5

And as both of the previous passages teach, many who have the image of godliness will be turned away. As we see, the Bible often talks about those who *do* have an actual relationship with Jesus yet do not believe that certain Biblical standards apply to them. Too many Christians have a *"form of godliness,"* yet deny the Truth of certain concepts, doctrines and absolute principles that are boldly written in black and white due to the fact that it may not agree with his or her opinion-based view of the Gospel. Nonetheless, one of the most important perceptions of God's character which we must all understand is this:

> . . . God our Saviour; Who will have all men to be saved, <u>and to come unto the knowledge of the truth</u>.
> —I Timothy 2:3-4

God does not care about your denominational background or preference, nor does He care about your opinion of the Gospel. Yes, He is able to have a relationship with anyone-anywhere, but He still desires that we all move forward and learn the deeper things written in His Word. This means that if we learn something deeper which can be supported by Scripture then we must act upon it. If we can understand that some organizations may be closer to the Truth than others then we must also realize this: We cannot afford to *settle* for the church we are presently attending if we know that something deeper is out there. As a matter of fact—don't miss this—if God gives someone a revelation of Truth and that person ignores, denies, or later turns his back on it, he is unfit for the Kingdom of God:

> . . . *No man, having put his hand to the plough, and looking back, is fit for the kingdom of God.*
> —Luke 9:62

It would be better for a person to have *never* known the way of righteousness if he later rejects it (II Peter 2:21). In fact, *when someone has been given much, much will be required in return* (Luke 12:48). If I did not believe "much is required" of me or that some of the issues I will be addressing pertain to our eternal destination then I would not be so persistent about sharing this with everyone. Furthermore, the things I have to say are not just my own personal interpretation of the Gospel. This is not just Andrew M. Denny's view or opinion of the Bible whereas . . .

> . . . no prophecy of the scripture is of any private interpretation.
> —II Peter 1:20

These things are commonly-known truths to a number of the saints of God throughout the globe and are boldly written in black and white just as the apostle Paul affirmed to us (II Cor 1:13). What I make mention of in this book was clearly taught by either Jesus Himself or the apostles (who were His witnesses). And anyone who claims to be a Christian should already know that we could never apply His Words enough, nor could we apply the teachings of the apostles too much in our lives. As a matter of fact, the more we live like Christ and follow the instructions in the epistles—even the instructions that today's modernized church says *"only applies to the early church"*—the closer we will be to God.

Whether you are a member of a particular denomination, Catholic, or any other church, I do not doubt that you are sincere in your walk with God. I could never tell a person *"you are not a Christian."* If a person has a relationship with Christ, then a person has a relationship with Christ; though, according to Jesus it will be evident to others whether or not we even know God (Matt 7:20, Luke 6:24). That's right! Our actions essentially prove to others whether we are actually living for God or just claiming to be "Christian." Nonetheless, anyone can communicate with God whether he is a part of a cultic organization or world religion. Again, God desires that we come to know truth no matter what our current belief may be or what background we may have (Acts 10:34-35, I Tim 2:3-4). So please understand that I do not doubt any person's relational status with God or level of sincerity as a Christian. That isn't the issue. What I do doubt, however, is whether or not everyone understands the truth about *salvation* to the same degree as the disciples.

Now, don't get the wrong idea. My goal here is to simply clear up a few common misconceptions. Something hard for people to accept is that they may not quite comprehend the teachings of the New Testament as well as the men who actually wrote the documents. For instance—and getting back to the plan of salvation—these days it is most commonly assumed that the way to be saved is to simply repeat the *"sinners prayer,"* or to, *"accept the Lord as your personal Savior,"* and instantly you are "saved." Nevertheless, what everyone must accept, which is something that itching ears must first realize, is this:

> ➤ *"Accepting the Lord"* as one's personal Savior will not automatically "save" anyone.
> ➤ Asking Jesus into your heart (*the sinner's prayer*) is not enough to get a person to Heaven.
> ➤ *"Believing on the Lord Jesus Christ"*—by itself—will not save you from an eternity in hell.

Hopefully *every* Christian today believes and accepts the fact that Jesus Christ is our Savior; nonetheless, accepting this fact alone does not determine one's salvation, nor did any of the apostles teach this concept to anyone. I do not wish to chastise anyone for believing these things; I mean that's probably all some people have ever known about salvation. These things are actually great starts, and I commend anyone who has taken these steps. But the fact is that none of the early church apostles taught new converts that these steps would instantly grant them eternal salvation. These ideas are the presumptions of man. There is more to salvation than simply accepting Christ into our lives. Salvation is a continual process (Rom 2:6, Phil 2:12, II Tim 3:14-15).

What everyone must accept is that it's possible for anyone who has a relationship with God to *not* know certain things about Him; even when it comes to salvation; even if he or she has been walking with the Lord for thirty years or more. Let's say a person who just happened to be raised Catholic is serving God sincerely and is applying his knowledge to the best of his ability. Does this mean Catholicism offers the most accurate doctrines of Christianity? Absolutely Not! When comparing the doctrines of Catholicism to those of the early apostolic era, hardly any agree. In fact, the Catholic Church has *added* more traditions to Christianity and *diminished* more doctrines over the past seventeen-hundred years than any organization under the Christian name. Yet God, who is willing to have a relationship with anyone-anywhere loves those who don't know any better, which brings us back to the point of discussion:

> . . . God our Saviour; Who will have all men to . . .
> come unto the knowledge of the truth.
> —I Timothy 2:3-4

God wants us to not only be saved but also to come to know Truth no matter what our current belief may be; no matter if we *assume* we are already saved. And the same principle applies to anyone who may be affiliated with any denomination. Another example of this can be observed by the circumstances of those who are unfamiliar with Pentecostalism (the infilling of the Holy Ghost with the evidence of speaking in tongues). There are many who may personally believe this experience was only meant for the early church. However, that doesn't change what the apostles actually taught regarding this promise. According to the following passage—in addition to the millions of witnesses today who have experienced and will testify—the infilling of the Holy Ghost is a promise for anyone interested:

> . . . and ye shall receive the gift of the Holy Ghost. For the promise is unto you, and to your children, <u>and to all that are afar off, even as many as the LORD our God shall call.</u>

> —Acts 2:38-39

Referring to both examples above (Catholicism and Pentacostalism); I used these two extremes for the purpose of proving a point. That being: no matter what denomination you may be a part of you must understand that there is always something deeper to the Gospel whether you may or may not agree. Just because you may not have seen something before does not mean that it doesn't apply to you. Just because your opinion may lean one direction does not mean it agrees with what the apostles actually taught. It simply depends on a person's Spiritual appetite; whether that person is hungry for Truth!

Since we will be addressing issues pertaining to salvation try to keep this in mind: *The areas that Satan is most likely to confuse the saints about are the areas that directly relate to the salvation of one's soul—that, and understanding who God truly is.* This involves the clarity of absolute doctrines of the Bible and discerning the difference between man-made traditions. We must understand that *deception* itself is more deceiving than we've come to realize because of how *rare* it is that a person realizes when he has *been* deceived. For those of us who already have the blessed assurance that Christianity (in general) is the one and only true belief system:

If we understand this then we must also realize that one of Satan's goals is to confuse the world about which *forms* of Christianity are closer to the Truth than others. Let's face it, of all the many different denominations, divisions, cults and other organizations that claim to be "Christian" yet preach diverse doctrines and follow various traditions, not everyone can be speaking the *absolute* truth.

Sadly, it seems like today's mindset is that some doctrines—though boldly written in the Bible—only apply to the early church and that our generation is not required to continue certain standards. Unfortunately, this mentality only sets boundaries in our spiritual walks and prevents us from achieving the very things we are capable of. The flaw with this assumption is that if we can say one thing *"applies to the early church only"* then we would be forced to say that everything applies to the early church only (aside from cultural differences which do not affect the Gospel Message itself). If we are not able to apply ALL of that which is offered throughout Scripture then why should we claim the Bible as our source of faith in the first place? If we claim to be a part of the same body as the men who wrote the New Testament then shouldn't we be applying everything they wrote to the churches? Absolutely! Nowhere in the Bible does it say that certain instructions apply to the early church *only*. On the contrary, many guidelines in the epistles are often concluded by further instructions to pass on the same customs to the next church. For instance, notice Paul's final instruction to the Colossians:

> And when this epistle is read among you, cause that it
> be read also in the church of the Laodiceans; and that
> ye likewise read the epistle from Laodicea.
> —Colossians 4:16

As you may have already noticed many Bible passages in this book are to confirm—and directly apply to—my own commentary, whereas some Scripture may be used hypothetically or rhetorically. Though some parts of Scripture—from the context in which it was written—may have been directed toward a specific group of people, this doesn't mean that it cannot apply in certain areas of others also. That's why we read the Bible in the first place—to apply it to ourselves! While I do understand that the audience of today's generation differs from that of the early apostolic era, the Word of God, which does not change, also guarantees that we have the capability of understanding anything (within our limits) if we truly have a hunger for God (Jer 29:13). That is why Paul instructed the churches to exchange letters; so they may apply everything and be of one mind. Paul's desire—as a God-ordained minister to establish the churches of God and teach the saints—was for every member of the body to follow his instructions, whether by word of mouth or by letter. Paul writes:

> Therefore, brethren, stand fast, and hold the traditions which ye have been taught, whether by word, <u>or our epistles</u>.
>
> —II Thessalonians 2:15

Quite frankly, if we believe that certain instructions in Scripture apply to the early churches *only* but not to Christians today then we cannot rightly say that the Bible is our source of our faith, whereas our opinions have more influence over us than the actual Word of God. In essence, how can we say that we are a part of the same body as the early church if we do not believe the same things or practice the same customs as they? How can we say that we are a part of the same church as the apostles if we are picking and choosing or explaining away specific guidelines throughout the Bible? In correlation, another demonstration of this can be observed by Paul's instruction to the church about gender-distinctive head coverings (I Cor 11:1-16), which act as a holy, outward symbol of submission unto God. In conclusion of this particular matter he writes:

> But if any man seem to be contentious, we have no custom, neither the churches of God.
>
> —I Corinthians 11:16

According to the passage above Paul believed there was no other custom for God's churches, whether anyone had a different opinion or not. Additionally, his guideline applies to *"the churches"* of God; not just one particular group; not just a particular generation or era; not just a particular geographical division. It is evident that—because he did not identify a particular small group or specific church—when Paul wrote *"the churches of God"* his instructions were addressed to anyone who is a part of any church under the Christian name; that is, anyone and everyone throughout the present dispensational period of humanity who *claims* to be a part of the body of Christ.

Don't get me wrong. I'm not at all implying that you're not a "true Christian" if you do not follow every single model throughout Scripture. I simply wish to reveal some of what the apostles actually believed and taught. Whether you want to follow these teachings; that is up to you alone. Again I will impart that when it comes to personal convictions—not doctrine—you alone must work out your own salvation with fear and trembling (Phil 2:12). Nevertheless, a person cannot go wrong by following the customs of the early church, whereas anything we do sacrificially for the Lord is considered to be a form of worship to Him. Obedience to God's Word more or less *defines* "worship." When we obey the instructions in the epistles we are obeying the Lord Himself. In fact, Paul writes:

> . . . the things that I write unto you are the commandments of the Lord.
> —I Corinthians 14:37

If we believe that certain guidelines in Scripture only applied to the early church then we would be forced to say that we are not accountable to the commandments of the Lord. Again, I'm not saying that any particular denomination is "failing" because they do not understand every single concept or model throughout the Bible. I'm just saying: Where Truth is . . . God is! When people truly respond to the commands that are boldly written in the Bible (rather than simply accepting the opinions of man), God will express His approval. This means that if you claim to be part of the true body of Christ your attitude should NOT be, *"I don't need to do 'this or that' to be a Christian; I've been 'saved' for years."* On the contrary, your attitude should be, *"What more can I do to be a stronger Christian? What deeper truths can I embrace? What have I been missing in my walk with God?"*

The statements above represent two types of people; those who have a hunger and want more; and those who do not. Most likely, those who *do* want more will acknowledge and apply much of what this book offers. Prime example: Acts 19:1-6 depicts a group of believers (which we will be discussing in greater detail) who came into contact with the Apostle Paul. Though they were *already* Christians who had previously accepted the Lord as their Savior, they did not let that stop them from embracing the deeper truths in which Paul offered. Hopefully many of you will be able to relate. If you desire to progress spiritually then you must believe that every portion of God's Word is true and that it applies directly to you personally.

On the other hand, those who are content in his or her spiritual journey and do not believe that *all* Scripture is profitable for doctrine and correction (II Tim 3:16)—or that the Bible applies to everyone—may just consider this book to be nothing more than a presumptuous yet interesting fictional work of art. No matter what type of person you may be, ultimately there is one certainty we must continually be aware of: *Satan's central goal is to deceive Christians into believing that certain issues pertaining to our salvation are actually of little importance and do not matter.* In other words, many Christians assume that some Heaven-or-hell issues are really not that serious in today's generation. I dare say that if you do not gain anything from this work then it is likely that applying godly principles has been a struggle for you in the past and will continue to be in the future. Let there be no doubt about it; this will truly be a challenging endeavor. Even so, I would ask that every one of you at least consider the following sections of this book in order that you may have the blessed assurance that you are walking in absolute Truth!

2

What Itching Ears Tend To Ignore

My people are destroyed for lack of knowledge: because thou hast rejected the knowledge, I will also reject thee, . . .

—Hosea 4:6

As the End Time approaches there are certain events in which the Lord Jesus Christ foretold. Many who study end-time prophecy are aware of predictions which have come to pass already. These same people—myself included—wait in suspense the more these events unfold whereas there are many fulfillments yet to come. Ground-breaking news continues to air daily with signs such as weather changes (earth-quake, tsunami, etc) and the formation of the one-world government. We continue to see more and more events which rock our world, ultimately setting the stage for the coming of the Lord. And while these examples are only a few minor instances, things are definitely happening!

But how in the world would we know about these things if we never read the news paper or turned on the television or radio to listen to the World News? How would we be able to determine that prophecy fulfillment is taking place if we neglected to observe the signs throughout the world around us? Would we gain as much insight if we chose to ignore these major fulfillments of prophecy? Absolutely not! Many would agree that—because of our awareness of end-time *SIGNS*—it is obvious that the "trumpet" (Rev 1:10) is becoming louder and more evident every day. And even though *no* man knows the day nor the hour of His return (Mark 13:32); for that reason we have the command to keep watch:

> *Watch therefore: for ye know not what hour your Lord doth come.*
> —Matthew 24:42

Even though we are unable to know the actual *time* of the Lords return we can be aware of the *season* through signs and predictions (Mk 13:29-30). However, this isn't really about end-time prophecy; moreover I wish to help you understand why it is important to take hold of as much information as possible to further understand Truth whether it involves the end, past, or present time details. We must understand warnings and predictions of the early church and what was foreseen to occur throughout the present dispensational period of mankind (the past two thousand years). We must have knowledge—or at least a minimum amount—of *world history* whereas it unveils much of why the world has progressed to the stage it is currently in. The more events we are aware of in the world, the more Scripture will come alive, as it was intended to do.

About the Network

For the word of God is quick, and powerful, . . .
—Hebrews 4:12

The usage of the word "quick" in the passage above is to describe how ALIVE God's Word is. (Some Bible versions even use the word "living".) As I mentioned in Chapter One my goal is to reveal exactly how the Word of God has worked as a Network in the world around us. And the passage above—in addition with II Timothy 3:16—is totally appropriate whereas it is the very mechanism and describes precisely what I am talking about. The Word of God is a living Network.

NETWORK: *a system in which two or more components—people or things—work together to accomplish a common goal.*

In essence, Jesus and His disciples worked together to accomplish a common goal, thusly illustrating how the Gospel has acted and is currently acting as a Network: The Gospel-Network. After Christ ascended into Heaven (Acts 1:9-11) the disciples (apostles) continued this Gospel-Network by establishing the churches abroad and spreading the Word of God. By the second century the apostle's ministry on earth had come to an end. Nevertheless, their writings—the Gospels, epistles, Revelation (the New Testament)—would live on. Therefore, we see even today that the Network, which is the Word of God (II Tim 3:16), continues to accomplish the goal; that being as follows:

> For the Son of man is come <u>to seek and to save</u> that which was lost.
> —Luke 19:10

Our purpose for living is to not only seek the Lord ourselves; it is to serve Him by seeking and saving others as well. Love God, love people (Mark 12:30-31)! We are to literally go out into the streets in order to compel others to come to the assembly (Luke 14:23). Much of our eternal reward is determined by the effort we have put forth in winning souls to the Lord. In fact, the Apostle Paul believed and taught that soul-winning plays a *major* role in our eternal inheritance (II Cor 5:10-11). Even though soul-winning *should be* common sense to every Christian, I dare say that most church members do not fully grasp the value or agree that it plays a part in our salvation. (Though soul-winning is a separate lesson in itself we must be reminded of what our expectations are as proclaimed Christians.) For now we must believe, or at least realize, just how relevant the Word of God is and how much the world intertwines and revolves around it.

Something to consider is what the Bible itself *is* (other than a network). It is a compilation of factual, historical records about actual people and places authored by prophets and eye-witnesses of the Lord Jesus Christ. Overall, the Bible is a series of real events. Nonetheless, Satan is devoted to veiling the truth from the world and will do anything—at all costs—to deceive us about the accuracy and dependability of the Bible. He will distort, defile, sugar-coat, veil, misconstrue, add to and diminish anything written in Scripture. This factor alone can be quite a stumbling-block whereas many have rejected God simply because they are convinced that there are contradictions throughout Scripture.

As Christians who read through the Bible regularly—or at least, Christians who *should be* reading regularly—we more than likely see many passages that we do not understand. Let's be honest. The Bible is HUGE, and from time to time we are going to see things that don't make sense; things that seem rather confusing. The problem, however, is that we too often ignore these parts of the Bible instead of focusing on them. People so easily accept that *"the Bible contains mysteries which cannot be understood"* and—because they've decided that's where the bus stops—fall short of achieving anything further. Still, what people don't realize is that the bus keeps on going. There is a reason why certain Biblical passages were written. The New Testament authors devoted their lives to spreading the knowledge of truth to the world through their writings.

A "Testament" is an authentic piece of evidence offered by a witness. It is a demonstration, a tribute, substantial verification; in other words, proof! If the Gospel was intended to *remain* a mystery to the world it wouldn't be called the New *Testament;* it would be titled *"Vague Obscurities of the Unknown."* While there are many references of the word "mystery" throughout the Bible it is apparent that—according to our hunger, humility, and willingness—we are *expected* to know and understand the mystery. As a matter of fact many references throughout Scripture actually guarantee that we *should* come to know the deeper truths of the Gospel. Take the words of Christ, for example:

*. . . Unto you it is given to know the mystery of the kingdom
of God:*

—Mark 4:11

We shouldn't think the mystery of the Gospel was intended
to *remain* a mystery. Even though a mystery is something the
finite mind cannot *fully* understand it is also something which
can only be revealed by the Spirit of Truth. We are to devote
our lives to accumulating these bits and pieces of Truth, which
will form a clearer picture of the mystery. Yes, the Gospel will
remain a mystery to those who do not *seek* Truth; however, the
Bible also informs us that it has been made known unto the
world (Romans 16:25-26). As Christians it is *our* responsibility
to get inside the minds of the men who actually wrote the New
Testament documents to better understand the Gospel; to have
a clearer picture of Christian truths. Even though the Sunday
morning messages we receive from our pastors may be absolutely
phenomenal and powerful we must not consider that in itself
enough to enlighten us of the deeper truths. Therefore, we must
at least consider the following:

➢ Ancient Culture
➢ Foreign Languages, including vernacular or colloquial speech
  (slang); the meanings of specific words in Greek and Hebrew
➢ Secular History (figures & events)
➢ More of the Bible itself (well, it's true; we *are* an
  under-educated generation, scripturally speaking). We all
  need to dig a little bit deeper more often!

We all have a promise from God:

And ye shall seek me, and find me, when ye shall search
for me with all your heart.

—Jeremiah 29:13

The questions we must ask ourselves (please don't skim over these questions):

➤ How hard are we searching?
➤ How often are we seeking?
➤ Where are we looking?

--------------------------------- † ---------------------------------

"Not My Tradition!"

. . . Thus have ye made the commandment of God of none effect by your own tradition.
—Matthew 15:6

Once upon a time a young lady decided that she would prepare a special ham for dinner—special in that it was the very recipe her great-grandmother used. As she proceeded to add the "sugar and spice and everything nice" she soon noticed a particular step in the directions which didn't make much sense to her. The recipe called for the young lady to *"Cut off a third of the ham before placing it in the broiling pan."* Confused, the young lady took a few moments trying to figure out why there would be such a bewildering step in the directions.

Nevertheless, because curiosity got the best of the young lady, before she followed through with the directions she called her mother and asked, *"Why does the recipe call for me to cut off a third of the ham before placing it in the broiling pan?"* Her mother responded, *"That's how granny has always done it, so that's how it needs to be done. You just make sure you follow after her!"*

But because the young lady was unsatisfied with her mother's response she called her grandmother to ask her the same question: *"Grandma, why does the recipe call for me to cut off a third of the ham before placing it in the broiling pan?"* Her grandmother responded,

"That's how mamma has always done it, so that's how it needs to be done. You just make sure you follow after her!"

Still, because the young lady was unsatisfied with her grandmother's response she called her great-grandmother to uncover the truth of the matter: *"Great-grandma, why does the recipe call for me to cut off a third of the ham before placing it in the broiling pan?"* Tickled, her great-grandmother responded,

"Darlin', the only reason I did that was because I never had a broiling pan big enough to fit a whole ham!"

This same principle—believe it or not—is very relevant even to Christians throughout the churches of today. Many believers do not have a clue as to *why* he or she believes certain doctrines. Generally it is because people tend to accept whatever they may have been raised to believe or what "the preacher" says rather than what may have actually been taught by the apostles. This is why it is so imperative that we confirm our current practices by referring to Scripture. If a certain Biblical passage seems to contradict or be in conflict with something we currently practice then we need to identify the cause. We as Christians—no matter what our denomination may be—need to know the origin of our current doctrinal belief. Notice what Paul writes to Timothy.

> But continue thou in the things which thou hast learned
> and hast been assured of, <u>knowing of whom thou hast
> learned them;</u>
> —II Timothy 3:14

We must understand not only *when* certain doctrines entered the world, we must also know *who* introduced these practices to the church—especially if we desire to know *why* we participate in certain traditions ourselves. Now, don't get the wrong idea. If certain traditions in our churches today were not present during the time of the early church it doesn't necessarily mean we are "wrong" (depending on the tradition). Yet to understand more clearly what the author's of the New Testament believed we must first consider what the early church would have been like without our current practices. Does that make sense? Allow me to elaborate.

If baby-dedications, for example, were not a common practice during the early church era (not to suggest that it's wrong) then we must at least take this into consideration in order to further understand the nature of an actual church meeting during this time. I realize it's been nearly two thousand years since the church was first established and that it's practically impossible for us to fully understand what everything would have been like. But that only means we've all got some studying to do! People wonder why there are so many different denominations in the world and how we got to our current stage while the answers await in our local libraries and on *educational* internet sites.

❖ The Network:

> For whatsoever things were written aforetime were written for our learning, . . .
>
> —Romans 15:4

Most likely everyone would say that it is important to know history. Nobody really argues against sending children to school to learn about the man who *"sailed the ocean blue in 1492."* Most people understand that by opening up text-books we begin to uncover and piece together exactly what brought the world to its present stage. The more we learn about factual events that have taken place, the more we will understand the overall picture of our existence. Unfortunately it seems that "Christians" tend to become less enthusiastic—even defensive—about certain historical facts that may threaten his or her particular religious tradition. The fact is that *all* churches practice some type or form of tradition that was not practiced by the early church. The questions we must ask ourselves:

➢ Can we afford to practice certain man-made traditions?
➢ Can we afford to neglect some of the early church customs?
➢ Have our modern traditions affected any of the Lord's commands?
➢ Do certain traditions affect our salvation?

Basically, the overall question is: *Which traditions are acceptable to God, and which ones are not?* In order to answer this we must first understand: it's *one* thing to practice unnecessary traditions for a good cause when we are not obligated to, but it's *another* thing to neglect certain practices that are *required* of us; practices that were mandated by Jesus and the apostles. It would be better on the Day of Judgment to hear Jesus say, *"You didn't really have to do all of that, but I appreciate your extra sacrificial effort"* than to risk hearing, *"I'm afraid your efforts were not enough; depart from Me, I never knew you"* (Matt 7:23). When we practice certain traditions which we are *not* obligated to we must be able to discern whether or not our practices are actually improper. In other words: If a manmade tradition compromises the integrity of sound doctrine then it is unacceptable and cannot be categorized as a *"useless controversy"* (Titus 3:9). To further set things into perspective I will use both *baby-dedications* and *infant-baptisms* as examples.

Baby-Dedication: if this had an effect on the message of salvation or an ordinance of God then it would definitely be an issue. However, because baby dedication is more or less the act of praying a blessing over an infant's life it is a good thing. Many examples in Scripture actually confirm that we are encouraged to pray for the well-being of others and to bless even our enemies (Luke 6:28, Rom 12:14, Col 1:9, I Th 5:25, II Th 1:11, Jas 5:16). And though baby dedication may not have been a common practice during this era, we do see patterns for this throughout Scripture (Luke 2:22-32).

On the other hand,

Infant-Baptism: though a highly recognized icon of Catholicism since it was mandated in approximately 400 AD, it is a tradition which has altered a covenant between the individual saint and God. Because water baptism is a *pledge* toward God (I Peter 3:21), one must choose for himself whether or not he will make this pledge. How can a person make a pledge to God when his guardian made this decision for him? Make sense?

The danger with traditions such as infant-baptism is that it distorts our perception of what was first presented as *true* Christianity. If a person goes through life assuming he is not accountable to the *command* of baptism because he was baptized as a baby then he misses the opportunity to make this pledge for himself. Moreover, because this tradition conflicts with a command of God it has absolutely no effect whatsoever (spiritually speaking); it's pointless!

> . . . *Thus have ye made the commandment of God of none effect by your own tradition. But in vain they do worship me, teaching for doctrines the commandments of men.*
> —Matthew 15:6, 9

When Jesus addressed this issue (manmade tradition) with the Pharisees He considered their own doctrines to be something which devalued God's ordinances. It was because of their preferred traditions that God's commandments became worthless. The passage above is very significant as to what the following chapters offer, whereas it will verify whether our own traditions today have made God's commands and covenants "of none effect." As we have observed already there are traditions in which are acceptable to God (baby dedications), whereas they do not conflict with His commandments; and then there are some that do (infant baptism).

One thing itching ears tend to ignore is that Jesus' conversations with the Pharisees were meant for us to observe and apply to ourselves even today. It foreshadows today's pharisaic Christian mainstream and her resistance to absolute doctrine. The general theme Jesus portrayed through His interaction with the Pharisees is for us to be willing to deny our own traditions in order to draw nigh unto Him. As you will see throughout the remainder of this book there is a vast similarity between the Pharisees of the New Testament and the *Pharisees of the modern-day churches*. Just as these "holier-than-thou's" truly believed they were in the will of God yet hindered others from receiving Truth, history repeats itself as we see this tragic reality today in the contemporary Christian society. The main thing to observe is that the Pharisees were too proud to admit they needed more; they could not find it in themselves to be humble before God. And in turn, Jesus informed them that they did not even know the God in whom they claimed to serve (John 8:47). Though offered the way of salvation the Pharisees unfortunately rejected it.

Yes, some traditions *are* more serious than others. When certain teachings influence the message of salvation or have an effect on the ordinances of God it is unacceptable. Something I will mention—and will mention again—is that, tampering with a covenant between God and man is an abomination. Altering or modifying an absolute principle of Christianity—or teaching that some commands are optional—is blasphemy. Not to imply that any particular church organization is preaching blasphemies *intentionally;* nonetheless, we must observe the secrets of the past to uncover how, when, where, and why the New Testament church drifted away. What itching ears tend to ignore is that the countless denominations in the world resulted from the *failures* of many; failure to abide in the apostles' doctrine; failure to uphold the absolute Truth. While the Bible teaches that we are to earnestly contend for the faith that was once *delivered unto the saints* (Jude 3), what we see today is that many assume they *are* doing so when actually they are defending tradition. Yet there is a difference between *defending* tradition and *contending* for the faith.

As for the contemporary churches: many would rather deny the reality of historical facts that disprove his or her current religious practice than to just accept that certain events took place. Still, we cannot afford to pretend like certain historical events never happened. Denial (or rejection) has cost too many their eternal rewards. If you believe that you don't need to know history in order to learn more about God then Wake Up! One of the devil's key methods of conspiring against us is by convincing us that we do not need to know certain aspects of history to be a Christian. Ironic, considering the fact that the Bible *is* a history book! Nonetheless, knowing history in addition with Scripture will unveil what has been going on behind the scenes. It will open up our spiritual eyes. I say this because one of the most common false assumptions among Christianity is that, *"History is insignificant because the Word of God is our authority."*

Don't get me wrong. The Word of God absolutely IS our authority; however, history should not be classified as insignificant or irrelevant in our perception of the Gospel—especially from a Christian perspective. Actually, the most common statement I've personally heard (from Christians), which is more or less the same statement above, is:

"I go by what the Bible says; I don't need to know history."

Yes, the Bible is our authority; however, much has happened over the past two millennia from the time the original New Testament manuscripts were written (including certain Scriptural alterations, which we will discuss). One very important and realistic detail in which the Bible constantly affirms through its numerous chronicles is this: *history has always repeated itself; there is nothing new under the sun* (Eccl 1:9-10). Overall, because there is a considerable amount of prophecy in Scripture—and because history is what fulfills prophecy—whoever claims they do not need to know history is more or less saying they do not need parts of the Bible. Much of Scripture is God's Word *foretold;* history is God's Word *fulfilled.*

Many Christians today assume they *do* believe what the Bible says; when in reality they believe an explanation of Scripture that was brought into the church years—even centuries—after the Bible was written. The apostles who wrote the New Testament manuscripts intended to convey a predetermined idea. However, because men have been changing the meaning of Scripture ever since it was written (II Pet 3:16), over the years many teachers of Christian faith have introduced alternative explanations of the Bible. Thusly—and this is the truth—many are only accustomed to man-made explanations of Scripture rather than what the authors actually proposed. What itching ears tend to ignore, nonetheless, are the *changes* and *additions* to the Gospel in which many of the well-known *apologists* of the second, third, and fourth century made to Christianity (which we will be examining in later chapters). While many assume that *"the Bible clearly teaches 'this or that'"* they have not stopped to consider whether or not the *apostles* believed or taught it. Though some ideas may *seem* to be Scriptural there are many that are actually extra-biblical delusions (remember this in Chapters 4 & 5).

Again, what Jesus and the apostles taught throughout the New Testament writings *is* our authority; yet what man brought into the church after the deaths of these men is just as important to know, whereas it shows us how and why the early church fell short. And because much of what helps us understand Truth is determined by knowing history, what we will be examining in later chapters—though only a few brief highlights—depicts some of the most monumental events that have directly affected what was first established by the Lord and confirmed by the apostles. For now we must understand the difference between the following:

> ➤ History is NOT: Personal opinionated interpretations, views, opinions or ideas of the Bible.
> ➤ History IS: Factual events; real people that have done real things throughout the course of time—some of which have affected the Gospel-Message.

Whatever we do we mustn't say, *"I don't need to know history because I go by the Bible."* A statement like this is nothing more than ignorance of the deeper truths of God's Word. Stating something like this only works against us in that it exemplifies our *unwillingness* to seek the Lord with all of our hearts (Jer 29:13). Furthermore, there are consequences for rejecting knowledge relevant to understanding the truth of the Gospel:

> My people are destroyed for lack of knowledge: because thou hast rejected the knowledge, I will also reject thee, that thou shalt be no priest to me: seeing thou hast forgotten the law of thy God, I will also forget thy children.
>
> —Hosea 4:6

One reason many will never understand the Truth to the degree of his or her full potential is because of the unwillingness to study; in other words, sluggishness. But again, the Bible says:

> Study to shew thyself approved unto God, . . .
>
> —II Timothy 2:15

How can we be approved unto God if we are not doing our duty of studying and learning? It takes action—demonstration to prove our love to God. This verse is not limited to Biblical text only. History in general—whether secular or religious—is documented for our insight. The Bible says *anything* and *everything* that was written is for our benefit. Again:

> For <u>whatsoever things</u> were written aforetime were written for our learning, . . .
>
> —Romans 15:4

Even though the Bible (in its original context) is our supreme authority we still need to know what has occurred throughout the existence of the world. As a matter of fact, since the Bible *is* our authority wouldn't that give us a good enough reason to accept the guidance in which the previous two passages dictate (studying and learning about the past)? Since we have only a limited time here on earth then maybe we as Christians shouldn't allow our lazy human nature to determine what our priorities should be. If we really want to call ourselves "Christians" then should we not die to our flesh more often by maintaining a daily walk seeking truth? Absolutely!

Think about this: We live in the age of *information* and *technology*. We have almost any and every topic of interest imaginable readily available at the click of a button. The *Internet*—because of its accessibility—has become the most popular and widely used device ever to uncover information. We have access to dictionaries, encyclopedias, Bible websites (including various studies, concordances, maps, and charts), current news articles, and even the most ancient historical archives. Yet because of our impulsiveness many would rather use this source for purposes other than gaining Spiritual knowledge. Isn't that a tragic irony? In the age of *Information & Technology* the majority would rather use the most *advanced* piece of technology for *useless* information (spiritually speaking). That's like having food in your hand but being too lazy to lift it to your mouth (Prov 19:24)! Nevertheless, Jesus informs us that those who remain busy shall be blessed:

> *Blessed is that servant, whom his lord when he cometh shall find so doing.*
>
> —Matthew 24:46

When Jesus returns His desire is that we will be busy DOING something to benefit His Kingdom. I remember hearing the following statement one Sunday morning during a very challenging sermon:

"If you want to hear 'Well done' then you will have to DO WELL!"

For starters, we must continually bury ourselves in God's Word to not only to feed ourselves, but also to train others in the faith. Second, we must have at least a minimum amount of historical knowledge in order to be able to explain some of the more controversial questions—questions such as:

> ➤ *"Why are there so many different types of churches in the world?"*
> ➤ *"Who started all of the different types of churches in the world?"*
> ➤ *"Why do some churches believe things that other churches do not?"*

Ask yourself: *"Can I answer any of the questions above appropriately?"* What itching ears tend to ignore are *these types of questions;* however these are very real questions. These types of questions can be tricky to answer if you do not know the origins of different beliefs. Consider the following question, which is probably the most controversial, yet requires the most speculation of all?

"Which church is the true church of God?"

Now, don't get the wrong idea. I'm not suggesting that there is only one group of people from a single church building who will make it to Heaven. That's not the point! What I am saying is that these are the types of questions in which the world demands an answer. Even though this question is commonly ignored by some of the most devout Christians, this is the very question that we need to be able to answer *appropriately,* whereas it shows forth much of what lost souls are curious about. We cannot afford to ignore any of these questions when souls are rejecting God because they do not understand these things. One reason this book was written is for the purpose of answering these questions in a way that makes sense to the lost (and unlearned Christians). We must realize something: there is more to spreading the Gospel than simply quoting John 3:16. We as Christians are commanded to have answers readily available for every type of question about our faith:

> . . . be ready always to give an answer to every man that asketh you a reason of the hope that is in you with meekness and fear:
>
> —I Peter 3:15

> Preach the word; be instant in season, out of season;
>
> —II Peter 4:2

Hopefully this has challenged you somewhat; nevertheless I'll go ahead and take this matter a step further by asking you to humbly consider the following passage:

> For when for the time ye ought to be teachers, ye have need that one teach you again . . .
>
> —Hebrews 5:12

If we are not spiritually mature enough to be teaching others then we are nothing more than blind guides leading the blind. If we are not continuing the apostle's doctrine while ministering to others then we are blind guides leading the blind. If we cannot answer the questions listed above appropriately then we are blind guides leading the blind. And if we are currently teaching doctrines in which we do not know the origin—if we are practicing man-made traditions that have taken the place of the commands of God—then we are blind guides leading the blind.

The Danger:

> . . . if the blind lead the blind, <u>both shall fall</u> into the ditch.
>
> —Matthew 15:14

In order to ensure that we ourselves are not *"the blind leading the blind"* we must validate whether or not our current traditions have affected any of the commands of God. We must know beyond a shadow of a doubt that *what* we are preaching is in accordance with the Word of God. Let there be no confusion; you (anyone) can have a relationship with Christ and still be blind to some of the most relevant truths of Christianity (Acts 19:1-6). The key factors, nonetheless, which determine the extent of what God will reveal to us, are summed up in the following three questions (from the introduction):

➢ How hungry are you (Jeremiah 29:13)?

➤ How humble are you (Psalm 69:32)?
➤ Are you "testing the spirits" (I John 4:1)?

One of the most important things we must realize is that God's desire for everyone is to be willing to lay aside his or her personal biases and opinions in order to advance spiritually. This means that no matter what denomination or religion we may have been raised in we must be humble enough to admit that we may not be as close to the truth as we assume. As a matter of fact there are multitudes of Christians that God has called out of the circumstances in which he or she was raised because they have come to know something deeper. There are many souls that have seen doctrinal inaccuracy in their church upbringing and—because they have identified the origin of their church's doctrine—have come to realize *why* they were raised to "cut off a third of the ham." The reason I offer the three questions above is because it's not easy to uncover doctrinal discrepancies of one's belief. These questions determine whether or not a person *will* progress spiritually and can be used to measure the height of his advancement.

Here's how:

➤ As for Question #1: The door leading to Truth is already wide open. But whether a person will enter depends on his *hunger* for Truth; how much effort he is willing to put forth to uncover it; where he is willing to look; how much time he is willing to spend doing so.
➤ Question #2: The *measure* of Truth one uncovers depends on the *humility* of the person; how much Truth the he is able to *handle* and being willing to admit that he doesn't have all the answers; being able to forsake his own opinion of Scripture and current traditions.
➤ Question #3: Depending on whether the person *"tests the spirits,"* he should be able to discern *fact* from *fiction*; whether it is God revealing Truth or the devils attempt to deceive him.

Whatever the case may be the person must come to a decision as to what he or she will accept as "absolute Truth." When a person receives a deeper revelation of God than what he is familiar with or was brought up to believe then he will be forced to choose between his *current* belief and *the path* that God is revealing to him. This can be difficult for some, whereas—and just to be more specific—many parents have shunned their children for leaving the churches in which they were raised. Even though some parents may not approve of their children branching out the fact is that any child who is called of God must be willing to compromise everything—even peace at home—in order to be accepted of God. Jesus said it Himself:

❖ The Network:

> *Think not that I am come to send peace on earth: I came not to send peace, but a sword. <u>For I am come to set a man at variance against his father, and the daughter against her mother, . . . And a man's foes shall be they of his own household</u>. He that loveth father or mother more than me is not worthy of me:*
> —Matthew 10:34-37

God calls people out from that which they may have ever known; no matter what they may have been raised to believe. His requirement for us is to be willing to compromise any human relationship in order to grow closer to Him. It doesn't necessarily mean that God's will is to set us at variance against our family, nor does it mean that some parents are "wrong" for raising their children under a certain doctrinal belief; it just means that God is always offering something deeper to anyone no matter what our spiritual level may be. What itching ears tend to ignore, however, is the voice of God as He attempts to reveal Himself to us more deeply.

I remember hearing a sermon in which my pastor titled *"The Seed of Sin."* While he intended on conveying an eye-opening message of conviction (which he did), much of what I retained came straight from the title. My conclusion: *"Get to the root of the problem; disclose the origins."* In relation to our discussion: overall, deeper revelations of Truth often come through recognizing the effect that modern traditions have had on the original Gospel Message; how certain man-made teachings have devalued the integrity of the apostles' doctrines; how worldly philosophies have consequently distorted our perceptions of the true Gospel of Jesus Christ. Unfortunately, whoever does not uphold what the apostles originally taught—according to the following verse—compromises his salvation:

> MOREOVER, brethren, I declare unto you the gospel which I preached unto you, which also ye have received, and wherein ye stand; <u>By which also ye are saved, if ye keep in memory what I preached unto you, unless ye have believed in vain</u>. For I delivered unto you first of all that which I also received, . . .
>
> —I Corinthians 15:1-3

According to the passage above, we can be saved if we believe the message in which the Apostle Paul received; the same message that was confirmed by the other apostles. It is the same message that was given to him directly by revelation from the Lord Jesus Christ Himself (Gal 1:12). And because of this, if we cling to a doctrine that Paul *did not* teach, or if we *do not* believe something he *did* teach then—according to the passage above—we believe in vain. Moreover, some traditions and doctrines could very well have an effect on our salvation. The Bible constantly instructs us to preach *everything* consistently with the apostles. Paul even states,

> If any man teach otherwise, and consent not to wholesome words, even the words of our Lord Jesus Christ, and to the doctrine which is according to godliness; He is proud, knowing nothing, . . . and destitute of the truth, . . .
>
> —I Timothy 6:3-5

Paul stated this knowing ahead of time that one day absolute truths of Christianity would be considered to be *heresy* (II Tim 3:5,7, 4:3-4). He also states that he dealt with *"false brethren"* throughout his ministry (II Cor 11:26). He recognized men who have *perverted* the Gospel of Christ (Gal 1:7). New Testament author, Jude comments that *certain men crept in unawares* or unnoticed (Jude 3). Overall, we see that the apostles *expected* false teaching (deception) to thrive among Christianity:

> But evil men and seducers shall wax worse and worse, deceiving, and being deceived.
> —II Timothy 3:13

Paul foresaw the effect that false teachers would have among Christianity. He knew there would come a day that Christians would appear to be godly yet would not accept the truth:

> Having a form of godliness, but denying the power thereof; . . . Ever learning, and never able to come to the knowledge of the truth.
> —II Timothy 3:5, 7

That is why he urged others to have knowledge of the true doctrine of Christ (II Tim 3:14-17). While it was foretold that Christians would one day heap to themselves false teachers who would deceive the church (II Tim 4:3-4), nobody seems to consider this to be a reality these days—even though the various denominations who preach diverse doctrines make it quite obvious. Modern Christianity so easily overlooks the division among faith and does not feel as though this issue is serious enough to address. Still, what itching ears tend to ignore are the constant *warnings* to the early churches of the very things which would result in denominationalism:

> Beware lest any man spoil you <u>through philosophy</u> and vain deceit, after the <u>tradition of men</u>, after the <u>rudiments of the world</u>, and not after Christ.
>
> —Colossians 2:8

What itching ears tend to ignore is any piece of information—whether it be true or false—that disagrees with his or her denominational code; anything that is inconsistent with his or her opinion of the Gospel; anything different from his or her preferred traditions; anything contrary to what he or she may have been raised to believe. Nevertheless, the Bible teaches that . . .

> . . . *whosoever he be of you that forsaketh not <u>all that he hath</u>, he cannot be my disciple.*
>
> —Luke 14:33

Should we not think that, because the passage above says we must be willing to forsake *everything*, this would include our personal opinions of the Gospel as well as our stubborn nature; in other words, our resistance to convicting challenges? While it is true that we are under grace through the New Covenant of salvation we must understand that this does not automatically permit us to believe whatever we want or to live however we please and still be saved. What itching ears tend to ignore is that the God we serve now is the same God we read about in the Old Testament.

I say this because among modern Christianity a typical and distorted view concerning those of the Old Covenant is that, *"because these individuals constantly underwent instant judgment upon breaking their commandments they must have therefore been held accountable to more since they were judged more strictly."* In other words, the typical mindset is that, *"God's judgment was more severe in the Old Testament; He was stricter then than He is now."* Modern Christianity tends to believe in a more lenient God these days and further rationalizes this perspective by using the phrase, *"We are saved by grace,"* while excluding any further effort to live godly. The problem, however, is that sin is so justified these days that so many do not even understand the weightiness of That which justifies us in the first place:

> But now hath he obtained a more excellent ministry, by how much also <u>he is the mediator of a better covenant,</u> which was established upon better promises.
>
> —Hebrews 8:6

Although we are under grace because of the blood of Jesus Christ, it is for that very reason we must understand that we are likely to be judged more strictly in the end than those whose atonement of sins came through a mere scapegoat. Because Jesus gave *Himself* to be the sacrifice for us (in place of something expendable) we must realize that the consequences of our actions as "Christians" will be more severe:

> Of how much sorer punishment, suppose ye, shall he be thought worthy, who hath trodden under foot the Son of God, and hath counted the blood of the covenant, wherewith he was sanctified, an unholy thing, and hath done despite unto the Spirit of grace?
>
> —Hebrews 10:29

And one of the most common ways we have all *"trampled the Son of God under foot"* is by insulting the Spirit of grace; in other words, taking God's grace in vain through our intentional sins and our sins of omission. Perhaps this is why the early churches were constantly warned about this (II Cor 6:1). Even so, keep these things in mind. Everything I have offered up to now has been laid as a foundation; it is means of preparing you for the following sections whereas some pieces of information may be difficult to grasp. Remember, Acts chapter two says: *"they that gladly received Peter's word"* were added to the Christian faith that day (Acts 2:41-47). Those who were humble and willing to consider that which God offered were the ones who in turn received it. It started with *humility*. And though we are *"saved by grace"* we must realize that we must hold up our end of the bargain in order to receive this grace, whereas the Bible teaches that . . .

> . . . God resisteth the proud, but giveth grace to <u>the humble</u>.
>
> —James 4:6

Simple enough! We receive God's grace if we are humble enough to accept and apply the same plan of salvation in which He entrusted to the apostles (Heb 2:3). Now, if you have endured this challenge up to this point then not only do I commend you, but also I must ask: Are you so in love with Truth that you would do anything to understand it more accurately, even humble yourself because your hunger for God outweighs your pride? By this I mean would you be willing to lay aside what you currently assume to be accurate if you knew there was a chance that something out there is closer to the Truth? If so then read on . . .

> . . . for he that cometh to God must believe that . . . he is a rewarder <u>of them that diligently seek him</u>.
>
> —Hebrews 11:6

3

Salvation Aforetime

Then he . . . fell down before Paul and Silas, And brought
them out, and said, Sirs, <u>what must I do to be saved</u>?
—Acts 16:28-29

Probably every person at some point in his or her life has
asked this same question. It is the single most important
question on planet earth. Even though I've heard a
number of responses to this question not every response can be
the correct one. God's Word teaches only ONE way to be saved,
which means we are obligated to preach it. Don't worry; I'm not
going to go into detail about personal convictions because, again,
you alone must . . .

. . . work out your own salvation with fear and trembling.
—Philippians 2:12

You alone must choose what steps you will take in order
to advance spiritually, and you must do so without comparing
yourself to others. I say this because too often Christians use the
passage above as a copout when faced with correction. The first
misconception we must tackle—or at least realize and accept before
we teach others about salvation—is that Philippians 2:12 does not
refer to doctrine. It refers to personal convictions, continuance
in the faith; in other words, acts of obedience unto God. It was
not written for people to think they can believe whatever they
want or to decide for themselves how to get to Heaven. True

doctrine does not change according to the individual's perception of the Gospel, whereas the Bible teaches that the Word of the Lord endures forever (Matt 24:35, Mark 13:31, Luke 21:33, I Pet 1:25). Unfortunately, among Christians the passage above is typically used more to justify one's stubbornness rather than to examine his or her spiritual position.

Nevertheless, the Bible is very specific about the doctrine of salvation. Overall, we must understand that there is a difference between *"personal convictions"* and *"absolute requirements"* of Christianity. This study is designed to understand what the apostles taught new converts immediately after they chose to *"believe on the Lord Jesus Christ."* It recognizes what the apostle's believed were absolutes of Christianity (Heb 6:1-2) and distinguishes these from what many today *assume* to be personal convictions (which also should not be neglected). Overall, there are commands for us to carry out in order to *gain* or *inherit* salvation, and then there are values to *sustain* us, which we learn along the way. Yet, as for the initial *plan* of salvation there was only one plan in which the apostles believed, taught, preached, confirmed, and frequently wrote about throughout the entire New Testament. So . . . what is that plan? What are the true primary steps toward salvation? What specific procedure did the apostles *constantly* urge new converts? *What must a person do to be saved?*

In order to answer this correctly we must observe the answer that was given the first time this question was asked. Many are presently aware that Simon-Peter is the disciple that Jesus used to address the world on the Day of Pentecost. But what many tend to overlook—and *have* overlooked over the years—is that Peter's announcement was more than just an average Sunday morning sermon; it was what he essentially concluded from Christ's commission. From Peter's understanding, what he offered to the crowd was *everything* a person needs to know *first* in order to "enter the Kingdom of God" (John 3:5). Peter's words would not only confirm what the Lord Jesus first spoke (Matt 28:19, Mark 16:16, Luke 24:47, John 3:5) but would also bind the New Covenant in Heaven (Matt 16:18-19). Frankly, this is one of the most critical points in our understanding. As a matter of fact, before we go any further we must all be in agreement that it was *Peter* to whom Jesus gave this authority. Notice the following words of the Lord as He elects Peter to launch the church:

> *And I say also unto thee, That thou art Peter, and upon this rock I will build my church; . . . And I will give unto thee the keys of the kingdom of heaven: and <u>whatsoever thou shalt bind on earth shall be bound in heaven</u>: . . .*
>
> —Matthew 16:18-19

According to Jesus, Peter is now elected to launch the very first church of God. He has been given the privilege of holding the keys to the Kingdom and the responsibility of binding the New Covenant in Heaven. Now, let's jump ahead to roughly over a week after Christ ascended into Heaven to the day when Peter would confirm and fulfill the Word of the Lord. It was the Day of Pentecost, and the apostles were filled with the Holy Spirit as a result of fervent prayer in one accord (Acts 2:1-4). Spectators (Jews, devout men) from all nations were dwelling in Jerusalem and were questioning the logic of the events taking place (Acts 2:5-13). Once Peter addressed the crowd with the powerful message of Christ, thusly enlightening them, the reality and conviction spurred these Jews into popping the big question:

> Now when they heard this, they were pricked in their heart, and said unto Peter and to the rest of the apostles, Men and brethren, <u>what shall we do</u>?
>
> —Acts 2:37

And this is it! Peter's response was the initial declaration (to all nations) of the fundamental steps toward salvation. His announcement would be the first time anyone had attempted to fulfill the Great Commission (Matt 28:18-20, Mark 16:15-18, Luke 24:46-49). Notice what he mentions as part of the procedure:

> Then Peter said unto them, Repent, and be baptized every
> one of you in the name of Jesus Christ for the remission
> of sins, and ye shall receive the gift of the Holy Ghost.
>
> —Acts 2:38

"Repent and be baptized in order to be forgiven, and receive the Holy Ghost."

Now, before you jump to any denominational conclusions please consider first WHY Peter mentioned these three things. The questions we now need to ask are: *Do these steps really pertain to OUR salvation, even today? And what significance do these three steps hold?* Well, we must first understand that Peter was addressing a crowd that was familiar with a different procedure; the Old Testament procedure, which required a mediator (the High Priest). The things we need to understand today are the same things these people in the crowd were already familiar with. Remember . . .

> . . . whatsoever things were written aforetime were
> written for our learning, . . .
>
> —Romans 15:4

Therefore, we must consider the fact that people, events, and procedures of the Old Testament are foreshadowing's of the New Testament. Most Christians should already be aware of animal sacrifice in the O.T. and how Jesus Christ (the Lamb of God) rendered Himself as the ultimate sacrifice and fulfillment of the New Covenant. Yet as for the three steps that would foreshadow repentance, baptism, and the infilling of the Holy Ghost, let's observe the *old* procedure of the High Priest (or feel free to reference the books of Exodus and Leviticus). His obligations consisted of the following:

➢ An *Animal Sacrifice* with the shedding of blood provided atonement for sin. Jesus Christ the Lamb of God is the sacrifice of the New Covenant (Heb 9:7, 14). His blood covers our sins through *confession/repentance* (I John 1:7).

This is what initially activates the process of having our sins *forgiven* (Eph 1:7).

➤ A *Washing* procedure at the laver was necessary before entering the Holy Place. The Priest would have to make sure he was washed clean so he would be presentable before God. While blood *covers* our sins, baptism is what *washes* those sins away (Acts 22:16). It releases us from our sins. We are made spotless (or blameless) through the washing of rebirth (Titus 3:5).

➤ A *Lamp-stand* (candlestick) was required for entrance into the Holy Place. Since the Holy Place was totally dark inside, the fire from the candlestick would bring light. This represents the Holy Ghost, as He is our Light. Our body is the temple (I Cor 6:19), and we need His light within us (Heb 9:8-9). Furthermore, we cannot see to live in this dark world without God's Spirit guiding us. The infilling of the Holy Ghost is absolutely essential in attaining salvation whereas it guarantees our eternal inheritance (II Cor 1:22, Eph 1:13-14) and is what quickens our mortal bodies (Rom 8:11-15).

When Simon-Peter declared the New Covenant to the world on the Day of Pentecost he was affirming to the Jews: *"You still have to go through an initial procedure; however, the steps are a little different."* Notice, this made perfect sense to the crowd as three thousand souls took heed to Peter's words and were instantly baptized (Acts 2:41).

Now, just for a moment consider this: Genesis 2:17 offers the first and only command in which mankind was required to acknowledged until after his fall: *"But of the tree of the knowledge of good and evil, thou shalt not eat of it: for in the day thou eatest thereof thou shalt surely die."* As I mentioned, and what many overlook, is that this was the *only* command for Adam and Eve to be mindful of—the only command in which God relayed the consequences should the command be broken. Nonetheless, Satan, who is the "deceiver", was able to mislead Adam and Eve into believing the Lord's command wasn't nearly as consequential as the Lord expounded. In fact, he tricked them into believing they were not obligated to obey this direct command of God by any means. Still, what must be observed is that, if the devil was able to misconstrue the one-and-only command in which mankind was accustomed to, then how much more possible would it be for him to twist the *many* commands in which we are held accountable today? I mean there is a wide range of commands for Satan to work with; therefore, if Adam and Eve were obligated to keep only one command and were tricked then perhaps it would be much easier for the devil to do so with the number of commands of the New Covenant. Make sense?

Even though most Christians are fully aware that Satan's first attempt to interact with humanity was for the purpose of deceiving us, the vast majority cannot accept that he is permitted to do the same today; *deceive us about salvation.* Considering that the first Biblical account of Satan's interaction with humanity teaches us about his cunning nature, should we not open our eyes to see whether he has confused us about the Salvation Plan in which we are held accountable today? I dare say that he has deceived most church denominations today into believing that we are not obligated to follow *all* three steps in which Peter bound in Heaven (*repentance, water baptism, Spirit baptism*).

Men and brethren, we mustn't be deceived. When it comes to the Plan of Salvation we must understand that altering a covenant between God and man (as Satan did in Genesis 3) is basically a way of overriding God's authoritative plan. Since we are all *priests* of the New Covenant (I Peter 2:5) should we not consider that there may be consequences for neglecting any command of God ourselves? Should we be so arrogant as to explain away or disregard the significance of the three steps Peter affirmed by simply repeating the common phrase *"we are saved by grace?"* Can we still be saved if we choose to resist Peter's words? Well, the Bible actually asks the same question:

How shall we escape, if we neglect so great salvation;
which at the first began to be spoken by the Lord, <u>and
was confirmed unto us by them that heard him</u>;

—Hebrews 2:3

How shall we escape if we neglect the plan in which Peter confirmed? As we continue to observe the words and actions of the apostles it becomes clear that none of these men believed in any other escape method than what Peter initially declared on the Day of Pentecost. Notice what the Apostle John wrote:

And there are three that bear witness in earth, the Spirit, and the water, and the blood: and these three agree in one.

—I John 5:8

➢ The Blood: confession and repentance (covering of sins)
➢ The Water: water baptism (washing away and release from sins)
➢ The Spirit: the infilling of the Holy Ghost (renewing of life)

Consider the "water" just for a moment. The book of Acts reports someone asking the Apostle Paul and Silas the same question which the crowd asked Peter on the Day of Pentecost; *"What must I do to be saved?"* Keep in mind that when they were asked this question they were in jail, and the man asking the question was a jailer. We see an amazing example of character on the jailer's behalf. This display of humility comes from a man whose position was above that of Paul and Silas, whereas these men were legally under subjection to the jailer. Despite the facts the jailer laid aside his personal biases—his opinion of God and what he believed about salvation—and humbly asked:

Sirs, what must I do to be saved? And they said, Believe on the Lord Jesus Christ, and thou shalt be saved, . . .

—Acts 16:31-32

What a response! *Believe on the Lord Jesus Christ and thou shalt be saved.* It sounds simple enough; however, this is where most Christians are confused about salvation. One of the most common misconceptions among Christianity is that the plan of salvation stops at this point. Though millions are able to quote this passage by heart, too many do not have a clue as to what the following verses of the story affirm. Look again. Does it really say that once you believe you are "instantly saved" or does it say *"thou shalt BE saved"*? The confusion on this matter is formed because the passage above is so often taken out of the context in which it was written. It should be obvious to everyone that we must first believe in our Savior before we take any further steps of obedience. Even the devils believe in God (James 2:19). But are they *saved?* Is Satan himself saved, he's a *believer?* NO, there's more to this wonderful plan. According to the Bible after Paul and Silas instructed the jailer to *"Believe on the Lord Jesus Christ,"* the story goes on. They *continued* to speak the Word of the Lord to the jailer (Acts 16:32). And after he listened to Paul and Silas . . .

> . . . he took them the same hour of the night, . . . <u>and was baptized,</u>
>
> —Acts 16:33

Could it be that when Paul continued to speak the Word of the Lord, he was explaining the importance of baptism? Absolutely! Why else would the jailer have known to be baptized immediately, during *"the same hour of the night"*? We must realize that there is always more to the story than what the devil would have us believe. While many today teach that baptism is nothing more than a *"public display of salvation,"* the truth is that the apostles believed baptism served many more purposes than just this (which we will further examine). Furthermore, if baptism was meant to serve as nothing more than a public display then why didn't the jailer and his family schedule a baptism for their friends to see? Why did they decide to be baptized immediately (at the hour of midnight)? Why was this so urgent? Could it be because it is an essential step of salvation? Absolutely, it's obvious! The fact is that the early church never so much as suggested scheduling a baptism for a later, more convenient date. In fact, we see that the act of baptism was so vital in the early church era that the apostles were *commanding* others to do such:

> And he commanded them to be baptized in the name of the Lord.
> —Acts 10:47-48

Already Saved?

> That if thou shalt confess with thy mouth the Lord Jesus, and shalt believe in thine heart that God hath raised him from the dead, thou shalt be saved.
> —Romans 10:9

I understand that many people consider themselves to be *already* saved, especially when the passage above is typically one of the only formulas used for salvation these days. If you were to ask the average, every-day pastor what the plan of salvation is he would likely take you to Romans 10:9. It seems this verse is what you would *expect* to hear from the vast majority of Christians if you were to ask them about salvation. Nonetheless, and as we previously discussed by observing the *full context* of Acts 16, the passage above, likewise, does not guarantee *instant* salvation. It does not assure us of *automatic* inheritance of our eternal reward. Again, it says, *"thou shalt BE"* saved. Believing on the Lord Jesus Christ and confessing this simply points us in the right direction. Nonetheless, we cannot afford to ignore our further instructions in Scripture. The fact is that Paul's statement in the following verse directly refutes and invalidates the instantaneous-salvation theory altogether, whereas he plainly writes . . .

> . . . for now is our salvation nearer than when we believed.
> —Romans 13:11

Though many assume salvation is something we have received already the passage above teaches that we are only *closer* now to receiving it. Believing on the Lord Jesus Christ is a great start; however, we have not yet inherited our eternal reward. The Bible teaches that salvation is something we must continually live and work out; something we must continually strive for "with fear and trembling" (Phil 2:12). Too often Christians emphasize single passages taken out of context and conclude that eternal salvation can be attained by following just one single Bible verse in particular. For instance, today many denominations focus on single phrases such as, *"Believe on the Lord Jesus Christ"* (Acts 16:31), *"Confess with your mouth that Jesus is Lord"* (Rom 10:9), *"Call upon the name of the Lord"* (Acts 2:21) or *"We are saved by grace"* (Eph 2:8).

Mainstream Christianity typically chooses from one of the previous phrases and teaches that you instantly receive salvation upon following just one of these verses. This mindset is the result of something called *"single-verse theology."* Single-verse theology is choosing a single concept from the Bible and revolving an entire doctrine around it. For instance, many assume that simply because the Bible uses the phrases *"saved by grace"* and *"justified by faith"* that we are not accountable to many other principles which also play a part in our salvation. Many assume that by simply professing one's faith in Christ determines our future salvation—that if we claim to be a Christian then we have already received our salvation. Unfortunately, by focusing on portions of Scripture while neglecting other passages we only distort our perceptions of salvation because we are not applying *all* of what Scripture teaches. We are basically picking and choosing which parts of the Bible we want to apply to ourselves. Consider the following Word:

> *Verily, verily, I say unto you, He that heareth my word, and believeth on him that sent me, hath everlasting life, and shall not come into condemnation; but is passed from death unto life.*
>
> —John 5:24

Now, if I were to explain the passage above in a way that is flattering to the itching ears of mankind I could say that, by simply *hearing* the Gospel being preached just once and *believing* what I hear is enough to grant me eternal life. Honestly, it would be easy for a person to walk away with this assumption by reading the passage above. Nevertheless, while many disregard *all* of God's Word and emphasize only portions of what He spoke, the fact is that Christ also affirms the following:

> *. . . Yea rather, blessed are they that hear the word of God, <u>and keep it</u>.*
>
> —Luke 11:28

> But be ye doers of the word, and not hearers only, deceiving your own selves.
>
> —James 1:22

We must not only hear and believe what God's Word teaches, but we must also put it into practice. This applies to all of God's Word; not just hearing the Gospel and believing; not just confessing; not just repenting or being baptized. This applies to all of the commands of God:

> *If ye love me, keep my commandments . . . . If a man love me, he will keep my words:*
>
> —John 14:15, 23

We have to understand something: none of us have made it to Heaven as of yet; we have not arrived to our eternal destination already. According to the Bible we are not *"saved"* from hell as we speak. Our sins may have been forgiven (depending on what steps we have already taken); nonetheless, I've never talked to anybody whose feet have already walked the streets of gold. The term *"saved"* gets thrown around so casually these days and has consequently affected so many individuals' perceptions of salvation. We must ask ourselves: *"WHAT exactly defines being*

SAVED?" When carefully examining the Bible it is apparent that not even the Apostle Paul considered himself to be *"already saved."* Look at what he writes (read this carefully):

> . . . yea, I judge not mine own self. For I know nothing by myself; <u>yet am I not hereby justified</u>: but he that judgeth me is the Lord. <u>Therefore judge nothing before the time, until the Lord come,</u> . . .
>
> —I Corinthians 4:3-5

Paul's conscience was clear, but he did not consider that in itself enough to make him innocent according to his own opinion. He was basically saying *"So far I have taken many steps toward God; nonetheless, Judgment Day is still to come, and I don't want to be too overconfident."* Likewise, if we overconfidently label ourselves as *"already saved"* then not only have we judged ourselves before the appointed time (vs. 5); we are basically denying that it is the Lord who determines our salvation. Paul was aware that *"whoever the Lord justified, He also glorified"* (Rom 8:30). Nevertheless, he still understood that *"It is GOD that justifieth"* (Rom 8:33). It is the Lord who knows the hearts of man (I Chr 28:9). Therefore, we mustn't make this determination prematurely—or at all for that matter—when it is for the Lord to decide.

Now let me be clear about something: just because we shouldn't be too overconfident does not mean we should be uncertain. Though we mustn't assume that we are *already* saved from hell because of grace, we do however have the *answer* to salvation by knowing and understanding the born-again plan. We are to *live out* our salvation. It is something we must continually strive for (I Cor 9:24-26, Phil 3:13-14). Since we have the choice to continually be obedient to the Lord we must make it a priority to observe His commands daily so we can know exactly *how* to be obedient to Him. If we continually live by the Word, like Christ, we can have assurance that we are on the right track. We can be confident on the Day of Judgment if we are continually obeying God's commands until the end (I John 2:28, II Tim 3:14-15). As

I stated earlier, continuance is one of the chief principles in which we will be focusing on. And as Jesus affirms, *"he that endureth to the end shall be saved"* (Mark 13:13).

The fact is that the Bible does not teach that there will be a point in time during our earthly lives where we have done enough for God; a point where nothing further is required of us. In fact, if we are saved from hell as of now then there is absolutely no point in going to church, praying, reading the Bible or obeying any of the Lord's commands whatsoever. Conversely, the Bible teaches that we are to give our entire lives to Christ in order to be saved:

> *For whosoever will save his life shall lose it: but whosoever will lose his life for my sake, the same shall save it.*
> —Luke 9:24

Moreover, if we want to call ourselves "saved" then it would be wise for every one of us to do a self-check to make sure we have obeyed—and are continually obeying—the commands of God (and baptism is an initial command). But does the Bible tell us that we can receive our inheritance before that day? Absolutely Not! Again, it is a *continual* process (II Tim 3:14). Though many will take the steps of justifying his or her sins through the blood of the Lamb, the fact is that too many will not take any further steps toward Christ or the initiative to do any works for Him. Even so, God will judge us according to *everything* we choose to do here on earth (Rev 20:13). While so many Christians overconfidently label themselves as "saved," the fact is the verdict has not yet been determined . . .

> For we must all appear before the judgment seat of Christ; that every one may receive the things done in his body, according to that he hath done, whether it be good or bad.
> —II Corinthians 5:10

Again, this book is not for the purpose of telling Christians *"You're not saved"*; it is for the purpose of telling Christians *"Just don't overconfidently assume that you have earned passage into God's Kingdom."* Again, there is a difference between having your sins forgiven and being saved from eternal damnation in hell. There is a difference between *"premature judgment"* and *"preparation for judgment."* Those who overconfidently say they are *"already saved"* have judged themselves prematurely. They have basically said, *"I've done enough to make it to Heaven and have already earned my salvation."* In fact, I am reminded of a dear friend, who, even though she was fully aware that she was backsliding (no longer living for God but running from Him), stated: *"Andy, I know I'm not living for God like I used to, but I'm still going to Heaven."* Unfortunately, though I hope she's right, I'm afraid nothing in Scripture teaches that we can just give up on God and still be saved, whereas . . .

> *. . . No man, having put his hand to the plough, and looking back, is fit for the kingdom of God.*
>
> —Luke 9:62

> Be not deceived; God is not mocked: for whatsoever a man soweth, that shall he also reap.
>
> —Galatians 6:7

> Take heed, brethren, lest there be in any of you an evil heart of unbelief, <u>in departing from the living God</u>.
>
> —Hebrews 3:12

> For it had been better for them not to have known the way of righteousness, than, after they have known it, to turn from the holy commandment delivered unto them.
>
> —II Peter 2:21

Friends, the Bible constantly forbids falling away (Heb ch 6, etc). Past works are not enough to save us if we fail to continue in the Lord by living up to that which He has instilled in us. Be mindful:

> For the gifts and calling of God are without repentance.
> —Romans 11:29

We must drill into our minds the vitality of the *gifts and calling of God*. If God has instilled assets within us to benefit His Kingdom, how dare we look back to Egypt during our journey to the Promised Land? Judgment Day is something we must constantly prepare for whereas salvation is determined by our *continual* performance (Rom 2:7). No doubt, the steps you have taken in the past are important; yet what you do in the future should always be the primary focal point of your spiritual journey (Gal 6:9). We should never be deceived into thinking we have done *enough* to be saved, especially when the Bible offers many examples of men who constantly suffered hardship after hardship simply because they were striving to live up to God's expectations.

Now how many of you can honestly say that you have suffered for the name of Christ to the degree of the apostles? I personally cannot. While we become offended so easily if someone refuses an invitation to church, we overlook the fact that Steven, for example, was stoned to death simply for preaching the Gospel (Acts 7).

The Apostle Paul, who, in my opinion, was the greatest of all apostles, was flogged numerous times, beaten with rods, stoned, shipwrecked three times, encountered bandits, dealt with false brethren, suffered hunger and thirst, weariness and pain, exposure to the cold, lack of clothing, while enduring through the daily pressures of the churches (II Cor 11:24-28). Though Paul suffered these things in order that others may simply hear the Gospel of Jesus Christ, many Christians today allow the "Welcome" sign on the church building to be the only form of outreach generated. (Let's not forget that Paul's example was meant for us to follow (I Cor 11:1).)

Consider Nathaniel once again (John 1:47-51). When Jesus met him face-to-face He was pleased with his lifestyle, yet He did not instantly grant him eternal life. Though Jesus commended Nathaniel for being a true Israelite Jesus still required more out of him. Likewise, even if God approves of the current state of our lives it does not mean that He won't expect more. For now we must understand that there are further obligations in our *daily* commitment to Christ (holy living, giving, soul-winning, etc). And just to be blunt, steady church attendance is not going to cut it! Just because you have maintained the routine of walking through the doors of the sanctuary for the past twenty years (even lifting your hands to God) does not mean you are "safe." First and foremost there must be no confusion about the basics. There must be a *"Born-Again"* experience!

Born Again

Verily, verily, I say unto thee, Except a man be born again, he cannot see the kingdom of God . . . . Verily, verily, I say unto thee, <u>Except a man be born of water and of the Spirit, he cannot enter into the kingdom of God</u>.
—John 3:3, 5

Now, before we continue we must again realize that, Satan, who works in our churches by contaminating the original apostolic doctrines, will do anything at all costs to misconstrue the meaning of the passage above. The reason is because it reveals our ticket into the Kingdom of God. While many have their own opinions as to what this verse *implies* we must all be in agreement that the apostles believed it holds only one *absolute* meaning. First and foremost it clearly states that unless we *do something*, we "cannot enter" into God's Kingdom. We must all agree—and frankly nobody should deny—that this is a matter of salvation. The apostles believed Jesus held the words to eternal life (John 6:68). But even though Jesus specifically mentions two important steps to take in order to enter the Kingdom of God today's denominational mainstream overlooks the confirmations of the apostles that fulfilled these words of Jesus.

I remember hearing a good friend of mine, Pastor Wayne A. Lawson, who presented the following suggestion as he delivered a very powerful message; a suggestion in which I personally hold as being legitimate. His statement: *"There are just too many churches in the world who quote John 3:16 so casually these days, but sadly they are oblivious to what the Bible says just a few verses prior"* (referring to John 3:5). Though John 3:5 is commonly overlooked by the vast majority it seems as if those who *do* acknowledge this verse have tried to explain away its meaning. Nevertheless, the following sections clearly illustrate what the apostles actually believed and taught concerning this issue. And for those of you who don't already know: the apostles believed that being born of the water and Spirit referred to *water-baptism* and the *baptism of the Holy Spirit*.

Before we dive into the confirming words and actions of the apostles first consider the topic of *Repentance*. People don't necessarily question what it means to repent of one's sins. Throughout many of the churches abroad it is commonly understood that the location in our church buildings near the foot of the platform is associated with the *altar of repentance*. We most commonly recognize the altar as being the place where hearts are changed; where people experience powerful conviction; where people come to acknowledge and respond to the voice of God. The altar is common sense to many and *should* be a part of every church under the "Christian" name (and if not then something is definitely lacking).

Even the secular mainstream seems to understand that in order to be a Christian one must confess his sins to God and change his way of living. In the words of my pastor as he pointed out one of the O.T. foreshadowing's of repentance: *"God has covered sins through animal sacrifice ever since he clothed Adam and Eve with coats of skins"* (Gen 3:21). And even though there are minor misunderstandings about the difference between *Confession* (admitting your sins and asking for forgiveness) and *Repentance* (turning from your former sinful ways of living) there is, for the most part, no confusion about whether we must face our sinful

Andrew M. Denny

nature in order to come to Christ. Most people understand that Jesus plainly stated:

I tell you, . . . except ye repent, ye shall all likewise perish.
—Luke 13:3

Still, because there is more to salvation than the initial decision to follow Christ and repent of our sins the devil would do anything to confuse us about the relevance of anything further. Consider the fact that the two following areas under discussion—baptism & the Holy Ghost—seem to have the most diverse range of explanations by the various churches throughout the world. Many explain the Water-Birth as being *"a physical birth from a mother's womb"* while others associate it to the water from Jesus' side as He hung on the cross. Many believe we are Born-of-the-Spirit automatically once we *"accept the Lord as our Savior,"* whereas others presume this alludes to *"the resurrection of our souls after our deaths."*

Whatever the case may be—even though these examples are based on assumption—the following sections only confirm that *none* of the apostles believed, taught, wrote about, or even so much as mentioned these suggestions. As you will see, the apostles believed being born of the water and Spirit referred to nothing other than water baptism and the infilling of the Holy Ghost. In fact, a good friend of mine and minister of the faith, Brother David K. Lainhart once related *Repentance, Baptism,* and the *infilling of the Holy Ghost* to "The Potter" analogy.

His thoughts:

"Just as a potter molds and shapes his clay into a pot, the Lord transforms us into His own vessels through Repentance. Once the pot is formed the potter will wash it to remove any excess material or stain. Likewise, the Lord removes every blemish within us through Baptism, making us spotless. Then, once the potter's vessel is ready to use, he is able to fill it with whatever he desires. As for the Lord, it is His desire to fill His vessels with His Spirit."

The Water

. . . eight souls were <u>saved by water</u>. The like figure
whereunto <u>even baptism doth also now save us</u> . . .
—I Peter 3:20-21

When viewing water baptism we shouldn't think that it
something to merely *consider* or schedule years down the road
after we repent and accept Jesus Christ as our Savior. The book of
Acts demonstrates that repentance and baptism were considered
to be a single-featured event. Likewise, we should make it a
priority to urge others to be baptized at the moment of his or her
conversion. We must follow in the steps of Christ as He showed
us the way by going through the procedure Himself (Mark 1:9).
As Christians who claim to be followers of Christ this act of
obedience would only be appropriate whereas Jesus taught His
disciples to do the same (John 3:22, 4:1-2). Even though many
churches today brush this matter aside and denote baptism as
"optional" we see from the words and actions of the apostles
that they simply laid their personal opinions aside and obeyed
the command of the Lord. They did not *add to* the command of
baptism, nor did they *diminish* from it; they simply submitted to
it. Furthermore, the Bible even teaches that we should not argue
about or question whether or not a person *"should or should not
be"* baptized. Notice Peter's approach as he urges another group of
believers to go through the procedure:

> <u>Can any man forbid water, that these should not be
> baptized</u>, which have received the Holy Ghost as well
> as we? And <u>he commanded them to be baptized</u> in the
> name of the Lord.
>
> —Acts 10:47-48

Quite frankly, to say that *"a person does not have to be baptized"*
is forbidding baptism, especially being a command of God. And
there is not one single passage throughout Scripture showing

that the apostles offered the "option" of baptism. During their ministry—whether a person had *already* received the Holy Ghost or not—they believed that if a person wanted to take part in the New Covenant of Salvation then he must undergo water baptism. These men believed baptism was absolutely a part of the born-again experience. In fact there are no other recorded teachings or events in the New Testament besides water baptism which could even faintly be associated with the water birth in which Jesus spoke of in John 3:5. *The apostles preached what they understood were matters of salvation.* They heard the following words proceed from the mouth of Jesus:

> He that believeth <u>and is baptized shall be saved</u>; but he that believeth not shall be damned.
> —Mark 16:16

Over the years many have tried to explain away what Jesus plainly stated in the passage above. (I've even been told by a so-called pastor that I *"shouldn't take this verse too literally."*) Another man suggested to me that Jesus was only talking about "some" Christians but not all. You see, man has twisted the original Gospel-Message by classifying baptism under the category of a *"personal conviction that one should* [merely] *consider"* rather than an absolute principle in which one *must* undergo. If there is any other explanation as to what Jesus meant by the phrase *"born of water"* (John 3:5) then it is not recorded in Scripture. We only see the *recurrent* water-baptisms throughout the New Testament. The problem with denoting water-baptism as "optional" is that it is an attempt to alter a covenant between God and man. By preaching that souls can still be saved even if they neglect certain commands then we are suggesting that God's ordinances have no authority. By explaining away the merit of water baptism we are . . .

> Making the word of God of none effect through your own tradition, which ye have delivered:
> —Mark 7:13

Now, let's be humble for a moment. If we expect to inherit eternal life without showing forth the willingness to obey a simple one-time command then I am afraid we are guilty of pride (Gal 6:3). And we should all know not to be too overconfident (see Matt 7:21-23). As Christians, the last thing we should consider ourselves is "deserving." Again, everyone has been given the command to be baptized. And the Bible plainly says that Jesus will only "save" those that choose to obey Him (Heb 5:9, II Thess 1:8-9). I understand that we are all human and we make mistakes daily. It is inevitable; we will fail from time to time. But if we cannot take five minutes of our lives to obey a simple one-time procedure then why should we expect to inherit anything from God?

> *And why call ye me, Lord, Lord, and do not the things which I say?*
>
> —Luke 6:46

Too many times we focus on ourselves without considering the reality that we may not be as deserving as we think. The fact is there are consequences for teaching that the command of baptism is optional:

> *Whosoever therefore shall break one of these least commandments, and shall teach men so, he shall be called the least in the kingdom of heaven:*
>
> —Matthew 5:19

Wouldn't it make sense that since baptism is one of the initial commands of receiving salvation that the passage above may apply? Absolutely! We don't consider any other command of God to be optional, so why should we assume the command of baptism is? It is because man has watered down the commands of God. Nonetheless, we are still able to see powerful parallels of water baptism throughout the Old Testament illustrating how it washes our sins away—parallels such as: Noah and the Ark, Moses and the Red Sea, and the priestly washing at the laver. In fact Leviticus chapter sixteen offers a very noteworthy foreshadowing of water baptism as it teaches us about Aaron's duties. Not only was Aaron required to sacrifice a goat for the atonement of sins, he was also commanded to use a live goat (the scapegoat) to release the people of his or her sins. The scapegoat would not only take on the peoples' sins, it would carry their sins away from the presence of God. You see, the blood provided forgiveness of sins while the live goat (symbolizing the water) granted them release of their sins. (In connection, the Amplified Bible even uses the word "release" while teaching the purpose for which baptism serves (see Acts 2:38).)

Though it does not determine salvation by itself, water baptism is a command in which plays a vital role in our salvation. Though some men teach contra wise, water baptism is more than a mere *public display* of one's salvation. From the very words of Jesus Himself and the apostles, we are able to substantially conclude—[please reference these]—that water baptism is:

- ➤ A *pledge* toward God (I Peter 3:21).
- ➤ The *union* between the saints (the bride) and the Bridegroom (Gal 3:27, Eph 5:25-27, see also Rev 19:7)
- ➤ The *burial* of the old, sinful self (Rom 6:3-4, Col 2:12)
- ➤ Part of becoming a child of God, being born again (John 3:5, Gal 3:26-27)
- ➤ The symbolic *washing* away of sins; *remission* (Luke 3:3; 24:47, Acts 2:38, 22:16, Titus 3:5, I Peter 3:20-21)
- ➤ A *covenant* between God and man; more specifically, an essential step or requirement of the New Covenant of Salvation (Matt 16:18-19, Mark 16:16, Luke 24:47, John 3:5, Acts 2:38-39)

The Spirit

Quench not the Spirit.

—I Thessalonians 5:19

I understand that the infilling of the Holy Ghost is actually a *promise* and a *gift* rather than a *command*. Nevertheless, it is the Lords desire that ALL should receive this gift. And as we previously examined, those who reject this promise "cannot enter into the Kingdom of God" (John 3:5). Though many try to explain away the reality of the infilling of the Holy Ghost the apostles believed this promise is for anybody that is interested; as many as the Lord calls (Acts 2:39). Sadly, many tend to search the Scriptures under the intent of *disproving* this reality rather than to *confirm* the promise.

Throughout time the denominational churches have offered a variety of explanations as to what the phrase *"born of the Spirit"* refers to, or to *whom* the infilling of the Holy Ghost applies, commonly explaining away the significance. Yet this attitude is totally backwards. Why should our objective be to disprove Christian doctrines which are undeniably written in the Bible when we should have the desire to confirm that these precious gifts still apply to our generation? The fact is that Scripture teaches that the true followers of Christ are those who are able to accept the more difficult teachings (John 6:53-69). I remember hearing something very impacting from Soul-harvester, Brother David Smith, whose suggestion becomes easily recognized once taken into consideration. His statement:

"There are three reasons why people will not receive the infilling of the Holy Ghost, . . ."

➢ *"They don't want it"*
➢ *"They don't know what it is"* (or fully comprehend the significance)
➢ *"They haven't truly repented"*

There is a great deal of truth to this. And from my own observation, the most common misconceptions and theories about the gift of the Holy Ghost these days is that:

> We do not *need* the baptism of the Holy Ghost in order to be saved
> The Holy Ghost is something we instantly receive upon confession; once we *"accept the Lord as our personal Savior"* (in which, if this were true, there would be no evidential sign of receiving it. You just have to *"take it by faith"*)
> The Holy Ghost was a gift for the early church only

Notice the words of Christ in which the Apostle John recorded followed by his own commentary:

> *He that believeth on me, as the scripture hath said, out of his belly shall flow rivers of living water,* (But this spake he of the Spirit, <u>which they that believe on him should receive</u>: . .
>
> —John 7:38-39

No doubt, we "should" receive the Spirit if we believe on Jesus Christ. But again, even the devils believe on the Lord Jesus Christ (James 2:19); are they filled with the Holy Spirit? Absolutely not! There is more to receiving than just believing! Now, as for the three most common misconceptions, I will begin with the latter and climb my way back up the list. If the infilling of the Holy Ghost was *"a gift for the early church only"* then why does the Bible plainly say it is for *"all that are afar off, even as many as the Lord will call?"*

> . . . ye shall receive the gift of the Holy Ghost. For the promise is unto you, and to your children, <u>and to all that are afar off, even as many as the Lord our God shall call</u>.
>
> —Acts 2:38-39

If you feel called of God then wouldn't you say this applies to you as well? The Apostle Peter, who bound this covenant in Heaven (Matt 16:17-18), believed this promise was for *anyone* called of God; anyone who claims to be a "Christian." Just for a moment consider how you may feel if you decided to offer a precious gift out of love to someone dear to you but in return they say, *"No thanks, I don't need your gift to be your friend."* Ouch!

As for misconception #2, which addresses those who believe the Holy Ghost is something we instantly receive upon confession and repentance; once we *"believe on the Lord Jesus Christ and accept Him as our Savior,"* (these usually believe there is no physical, visual, or audible sign or evidential confirmation that a person has received the gift): the following Scripture should be an eye-opener.

> . . . Paul having passed through the upper coasts came to Ephesus: and finding certain disciples, He said unto them, <u>Have ye received the Holy Ghost since ye believed</u>? And they said unto him, <u>We have not so much as heard whether there be any Holy Ghost</u>.
> —Acts 19:1-2

Did you catch that? These "believers" had already accepted the Lord as their personal Savior. They were already "Christians" yet had not even heard about the Holy Ghost. How can we say that a person instantly receives the Holy Ghost upon confession when the Bible refutes this presumption as these disciples contradicted this theory? (Remember this group of believers throughout the remainder of the book. Much of what we will cover is based upon this story.) And here is where the rubber meets the road:

> And when Paul laid his hands upon them, the Holy Ghost came on them; and they spake with tongues, and prophesied.
> —Acts 19:6

Notice what happened when they received the Holy Spirit? They spoke in tongues! While it is commonly assumed that, *"You DON'T have to speak in tongues to have the Holy Ghost,"* the Bible actually teaches that, speaking in tongues is *how you will know* someone has received the Holy Ghost (Mark 16:17, Acts 2:4, 10:44-46). It is the *evidence* that a person has received the gift:

> Wherefore tongues are for a sign, not to them that believe, but to them that believe not:
> —I Corinthians 14:22

And apparently this evidential sign was so impressive during one incident that a spectator offered the apostles money for this power (Acts 8:14-19). Still another common misconception is that "tongues" is only a gift for some, but not all. Yet there is a difference between the GIFT of tongues (I Cor 12:4-11), and the self-edifying tongue (I Cor 14:4). One form of tongues is for the purpose of edifying the church and requires interpretation (though not everyone will receive this gift); whereas the other tongue is for personal worship and should be practiced by all who receive the Holy Ghost. Furthermore, while many hold to the notion that tongues was solely for the purpose of enlightening the Jews in their own language on the Day of Pentecost, the references listed above affirm that tongues is not limited to this single event. While many deny the authenticity of speaking in tongues and explain away the reality of it all, the Bible commands us all to . . .

> . . . forbid not to speak with tongues.
> —I Corinthians 14:39

But since the topic of *tongues* in itself is another lengthy Bible study, let us conclude the matter by discussing misconception #1: *"You do not need the Holy Ghost in order to be saved"*. While many Scriptures refute this theory, I will begin by reminding you of what Jesus said in John 3:5: *"Unless a man be born of the Spirit, he cannot enter into the Kingdom of God."* Now, since the Holy Spirit is something we need to be "born of" in order to enter the Kingdom of God, then why would a person assume they can still be "saved" without it? How else can our mortal bodies be quickened at the resurrection (Rom 8:11, I Thess 4:16-17)? More to the point, who *wouldn't* want the gift of the Holy Ghost? Not only is this a gift, but also a blessing that comes with the POWER of God:

> *But ye shall receive power, after that the Holy Ghost has come upon you:*
>
> —Acts 1:8

How do we expect to perform healings or cast out devils (Mark 16:17-18, John 14:12) if we do not have the power to do so? While the Bible teaches that the Holy Ghost is one of the determining factors and is what guarantees that we will receive an eternal inheritance (Eph 1:13-14), this is where the faith of many is tested. Numbers of Christians serve God in many fashions yet cannot accept the major truths about Him (including the power of the Holy Ghost):

> Having a form of godliness, but <u>denying the power</u> thereof: from such turn away.
>
> —II Timothy 3:5

Today, the majority of denominational churches have a form of godliness; however, most do not agree that the infilling of the Holy Ghost is pertinent in this generation. Unfortunately, because the Bible teaches that the things which the apostles have written in the Bible are the commandments of God (I Cor 14:37), those who disagree with or disregard what these men affirmed actually disregard the Lord Himself (I Thess 4:8). The fact is that being filled with God's Holy Spirit essentially determines whether we are His children or not:

> The Spirit itself beareth witness with our spirit, that we are the children of God:
>
> —Romans 8:16

Just like refusing the step of baptism there are consequences for resisting the Powers and Ordinances of God, whether it be our subjection to earthly magistrates or God's illustration of power manifested through the Holy Ghost:

> Whosoever therefore resisteth the power, resisteth the ordinance of God: and they that resist shall receive to themselves damnation.
>
> —Romans 13:2

The Confirmations

Wouldn't it only make sense that—since being born of the water and Spirit is our ticket into the Kingdom of God—Christians might want to spend a little more time teaching (or at least studying and learning) about this subject rather than ignoring, denying, or explaining away the reality of it? The men who wrote the New Testament—which includes the words of Jesus in John 3:5—believed the born-again experience was a matter of salvation. Therefore, we cannot afford to neglect the recurrent actions taken by these men or the words in which they repeatedly spoke. That is why the Bible asks: *How shall we escape if we neglect so great salvation, which at the first began to be spoken by the Lord and was confirmed by them that heard him* (Heb 2:3).

Ask yourself: *"What were the actions taken by the apostles, which fulfilled the words of Jesus?"* If the plan of salvation was first spoken by the Lord and later confirmed by the apostles then shouldn't we at least consider the *repeated* events in the book of Acts? When truly observing and rightly dividing the book of Acts, it is undeniable that the ONLY scenarios which could even *remotely* be related to water & Spirit births are the constant, baptisms and infillings of the Holy Ghost. Any other opinion or explanation would be inconsistent with the apostles' interpretations. If the water and Spirit births pertained to anything else then the apostles would have confirmed it—it would have been written in the Book of Acts or the epistles. Yet NOTHING in the New Testament fits the description or lines up with the phrase *"born of water and of the Spirit"* more than the recurrent water baptisms and the baptisms of the Holy Ghost! Observe the following:

> ➤ The Apostle Paul's conversion (Acts 9:17-18). He was born of the *water* and of the *Spirit*.
> ➤ Cornelius made the same decision as well (Acts 10:44-48); born of the *water* and *Spirit*.
> ➤ A group of new converts in Samaria also went through the born-again procedure (Acts 8:14-17); *water* and *Spirit*.
> ➤ The group of believers (John's disciples) Paul came into contact with (Acts 19:1-6); they were born of the *water* and *Spirit*.
> ➤ Let's not forget the initial declaration itself (Acts 2:38); quoted by Peter, whose words were bound in Heaven (Matt 16:18-19).

Overriding Obedience through Faith & Grace?

For by grace are ye saved through faith; and that not of yourselves: it is the gift of God:

—Ephesians 2:8

While many quote the passage above so casually these days, consequently it has affected many into assuming they are *"saved by faith"* and *"covered by grace"* whether or not they have taken any steps toward God at all, regardless of what kind of lifestyle they may lead. As we discussed, many people have their own explanations of the phrase *"born of the water and of the Spirit."* However, we should not assume—and it's unbiblical to think—that we are deserving of God's grace while ignoring and resisting His commands and gifts. If this *were* true then—[don't miss this]—we would be able to preach that *Repentance* is optional. I mean, if nothing is required of *us* to be saved then what's the point? Make sense? Obedience plays a major role in receiving God's grace. As a matter of fact obedience is the key factor in receiving much of the grace God intends for us:

> . . . we have received grace and apostleship, <u>for obedience</u> to the faith . . .
> —Romans 1:5

Look again. Why have we received grace? For obedience! If grace were the only thing we were to rely upon in order to receive salvation then there would be no cause for us to live for God or obey His commands. The Apostle Paul considered grace to be something we should not expect, something unearned. In fact, he informs us that because God has *already* bestowed a portion of His grace upon us; for that reason we should devote our lives to obeying His commands more faithfully:

> But by the grace of God I am what I am: and his grace which was bestowed upon me was not in vain; but I labored more abundantly than they all:
> —I Corinthians 15:10

Everyone has faith in something. You must ask yourself what the phrase *"saved by grace through faith"* applies to. Faith in what? Does it mean that we must have faith in God's existence only; or faith that Jesus was raised from the dead only; faith in steady church attendance and being a "good person" only? Or could this be about faith in *everything* commanded by the Lord and confirmed by the apostles—including the actual *plan* of salvation (Acts 2:38: *repentance, baptism, Holy Ghost*). Over the years people have watered down the commands of God by stating *"We are saved by grace"* and leaving it at that. However, the Bible affirms that our faith is useless without putting forth effort:

> Even so faith, if it hath not works, is dead, being alone.
> —James 2:17

We all probably have different ideas or opinions of what exactly classifies something as a "work." Some people argue that *"baptism is a work"* . . . and since *"works will not save us"* . . . *"we are not obligated to be baptized."* However, we must understand first and foremost that baptism is more of an act of submission; a step of faith. In fact, Paul differentiates "works" from the act of water baptism:

> Not by works of righteousness which we have done, but according to his mercy he saved us, by the washing of regeneration, and renewing of the Holy Ghost;
> —Titus 3:5

Whether you want to classify baptism under the "works" category or not, it is an initial act of faith in which Jesus specifically commanded everyone to accept and obey; that is, if a person wants to be saved (Mark 16:16). And if we as Christians do not have the faith to believe that obedience to God's commands plays a part in our salvation then we have an even bigger problem. As Christians our primary focus in life should be to make sure that our obedience outweighs our defiance to God's commands, whereas the Bible warns us:

> For the time is come that judgment must begin at the house of God: and if it first begin at us, what shall the end be of them that obey not the gospel of God?
> —I Peter 4:17

While works *alone* will not save us, the fact is that we cannot be saved without some type of effort involved on our part. In essence and to further clarify what I mean, if a person has faith in the resurrection of Jesus Christ this is a great start. If he has faith in Christ's doctrine—that repentance and water baptism will remit his sins—this is even better. But if he does not take the time to actually repent or undergo water baptism himself then what good will his faith do him? Unfortunately his sins cannot be justified without some type of action involved on his part.

> Ye see then how that by works a man is justified, and
> not by faith only.
>
> —James 2:24

The phrase, *"Works won't save you"* refers to those, who assume they can make it to Heaven through their own efforts. Actually, the Bible teaches that we are *judged* by our works (Rev 20:13); how busy we remain; if we have obeyed the commands of God; whether or not we have won any souls; or if we have lived a holy and separated life; etc. The fact is that we serve a God who will render to every one of us according to our deeds (Rom 2:6).

The phrase *"Works won't save you"* derived from Ephesians 2:8-9 which states *"For by grace ye are saved through faith . . . Not of works."* However, in its full context we find that the following verse affirms that *"we are His workmanship, created in Christ Jesus to do good works, which God prepared for us to do"* (Eph 2:10). This passage (vs. 8-9) has been misconstrued and turned into wantonness by Christians in attempts to justify our resistance to God's commands. It seems as though people love to use this phrase as a copout when challenged to do something more for God; even if it is something as simple as obeying a one-time command (baptism). Many argue that Abraham was justified by his faith *alone* and that works had nothing to do with it. While it is *true* that he was justified by his faith, he was still tested to see whether or not he had any faith at all. In fact, we read in James that it was the result of *both* his faith and works which justified him (James 2:21-23). The reason is because there must be evidence that a person actually does have faith, which comes through actions of obedience to the Lord. In Truth, if a person has any faith at all then there is no question of whether he is willing to complete any works of righteousness or obey acts of faith or submission. Nothing will ever emit the fact that faith without works is still dead (James 2:17), whereas our works essentially prove whether or not we even have faith:

> . . . shew me thy faith without thy works, and I will
> shew thee my faith <u>by my works</u>.
>
> —James 2:18

Yes, *faith* is essentially the main ingredient in the justification of our sins and is what plays the most vital role in our salvation; nonetheless it is our works that cooperate with and confirm whether we even have faith at all. In other words, faith is the *saving* factor while our works are the *facilitating* factor, both accessing and allowing justification to be possible. In essence, faith is ineffective without works, whereas our works complete our faith:

> Seest thou how faith wrought with his works, and by works was faith made perfect?
>
> —James 2:22

---------------------------------- † ----------------------------------

Let's revisit the group of believers in Acts 19:1-6 (please reread if necessary). These people were—just as it says—believers. They were living a life seeking Truth and could appropriately be called "Christians." Still, even though these believers had already chosen the Christian path they needed to undergo both baptisms of the New Covenant. And when Paul informed them of these principles they did not resist the Truth of the matter. They did not question Paul or try to analyze the situation by looking for excuses as to why these things did not apply to them. We see an amazing example of character on their behalf. Even though they had previously become followers of Christ they still humbly accepted the reality of what Paul preached, thusly fulfilling what Jesus declared in John 3:5.

The reason I will be referring to the Christians in Acts 19 so frequently is because this story applies to the majority of claimed Christians in the world today. Like these early Christians, there are many today who are sincere and honest, who also may have been in church their whole lives, yet have not gone through the born-again procedure. However, a major difference between these early Christians (Acts 19) and many Christians today is the attitude. While these early Christians were willing to obey the Gospel-Message in which Paul preached, many today—having the typical mindset of complacency—tend to become defensive when confronted about salvation; assuming they have done enough or that they are "already saved." Too many of us have the mindset: *"You can't tell me I'm wrong; I've been a Christian for years."* Too many of us can't accept that we do not understand as much about the Gospel as we've assumed our whole lives.

Nonetheless, as proclaimed Christians—no matter what our denominational code may be or the steps we have already taken—must open our spiritual eyes to see what is happening in the world around us.

❖ The Network:

> For the time will come when they will not endure sound doctrine; but after their own lusts shall they heap to themselves teachers, having itching ears; And they shall turn away their ears from the truth, and shall be turned unto fables.
>
> —II Timothy 4:3

I'm sure this chapter has caused many of you to analyze or at least try to make sense of how there can be so many Christians in the world that don't teach the born-again plan as the apostles did. Ultimately, some of the questions you may have—along with other conclusions as to what this chapter is implying—would probably be:

➤ *"Apparently, many of the people in my church (possibly everyone, including myself) are going to hell because we have not been baptized or filled with the Holy Ghost, right?"*
➤ *"The majority of denominational churches do not teach the born-again plan the same as the apostles. Does this mean they are all going to hell also?"*
➤ *"What about the people that don't know about this plan? Will God hold some people accountable, but not others?"*
➤ *"How can God send people to hell just because they didn't totally understand the Gospel?"*

First of all, none of this should be mistaken as condemnation or judgment, whereas we will be judged not only by the measure of knowledge we have obtained (II Peter 2:21) but also how we have applied it (Luke 12:48). Although because of this factor alone we cannot afford to ignore some of the things in which we are presently learning, whereas the Bible teaches that if any man puts his hand to the plough and looks back is unfit for the Kingdom of God (Luke 9:62).

It's true that there are many genuine Christians who don't fully understand what it means to be born again. And I personally doubt that God, who is just, would condemn a person to hell for something he or she did not know. But that is not for me to decide. And quite frankly, the Bible does not teach that grace will override our ignorance to God's ordinances. In fact, it teaches quite the opposite (Heb 2:3). Yet at the same time God would love to see these same souls come unto the knowledge of Truth and submit to this reality so that he or she does not have to risk it. As for us: instead of trying to figure out how people can still make it to Heaven without going through the procedure, our responsibility, like Paul, is not to worry about whether people *already* know; it is to simply tell people about it! We cannot afford to analyze or rationalize God's judgment; we can only trust that God is just (I John 1:9, Rev 15:3). As a matter of fact, the Bible even teaches us to *not* question who will go to Heaven or hell:

> Say not in thine heart, Who shall ascend into heaven? . . .
> Or, Who shall descend into the deep? . . .
> —Romans 10:6-7

Too often we rationalize the circumstances of peoples' lives and try to determine his or her judgment based on what we know of them when we should be laying aside our personal opinions and just relay what the Bible says. I truly do hope that God's grace will cover a multitude of ignorance, neglect, sluggishness, and denial. But the fact is that nothing in the Bible teaches this, nor did the apostles assume this. Paul knew that there were sincere Christians in the world who did not understand everything about salvation, yet he did not question the logic or try to understand God's judgment. He simply preached the born-again plan because he knew that "neglecting so great salvation" wasn't worth the risk. Likewise, let's just leave judgment up to God. After all, He is just. He will render to every man according to what he has done here on earth whether he accepts the born-again plan or not; whether he understands that he must continually work out his salvation with fear and trembling or whether he assumes that he is "already saved." Furthermore, this book was not written for the purpose of determining who's saved and who's not; it is to reveal that there are too many churches under the "Christian" name that do not offer the plan of salvation which was:

➤ First spoken by the Lord (Mk 16:16, Luke 24:47, Jn 3:5)
➤ Confirmed by the men that heard Him (Acts 2:38; 19:1-6, etc)
➤ Bound in Heaven (Matt 16:18-19 and Acts 2:38)
➤ Repeatedly affirmed throughout the history of the early apostolic era (Acts 2:38-39; 8:14-17; 9:17-18; 10:44-48; 19:1-6)

For those of us who have the desire of understanding Truth more clearly, I have said it before and will say it again: if we were to teach that baptism or the infilling of the Holy Ghost is "optional" then we would be offering an alternative to God's ordinance; an extra-Biblical teaching; something that none of the apostles ever said. And since there is only one covenant bound in Heaven we cannot afford to present alternatives. God does not make exceptions according to status; He does not play favorites (Acts 10:34). He accepts those who do His will (Acts 10:35). Just because some of us want to simply ignore this reality does not mean that God will renounce what He has established.

It is all too common to hear Christians say, *"My pastor says 'such-n-such' and I know he's right."* Nonetheless, even though "Joe-Preacher" may say "this-or-that" we must ask ourselves, *"What does the Bible say?"* What was constantly taught throughout the New Testament? Can anybody actually deny that repentance, baptism, and the infilling of the Holy Ghost is what the apostles pre-mandated before any of our pastors took the pulpit? It was the first thing Peter mentioned during the establishment of the church when he declared the New Covenant to the world, and it is what we see spoken of so often throughout the New Testament writings. Salvation comes not only through *believing* but through obedience to the born-again plan:

> . . . he saved us, by the washing of regeneration, and renewing of the Holy Ghost;
>
> —Titus 3:5

Again, can anyone actually suggest that baptism or the infilling of the Holy Ghost is not essential in gaining salvation? If so then we are more or less saying the plan in which the apostles constantly urged does not apply to us. Given that Jesus Christ is the same yesterday, today, and forever (Heb 13:8), why should anyone who claims to be a Christian believe that this particular part of the Message was only meant to be taught during the early church ministry? When we analyze or try to justify whether or not certain doctrines apply to us today, not only does it demonstrate that we question the Lord's judgment, it also reveals the level of *willingness* (or unwillingness, I should say) to simply obey the commands of God. What it all boils down to is this: if we truly love God then we will not look for excuses as to why certain promises and ordinances do not apply to us. We will do whatever we can, at all costs, to accept and apply *anything* that God offers; *anything* written in the Word of God; *anything* taught by the apostles.

Men and brethren, we must not look for excuses or error in this plan. Like the believers in Acts 19:1-6, we too must except it and realize that nobody is exempt from it. Everything we may think we already know could be contrary to what the apostles actually taught; what the Word of God actually says. Just because we may have heard something contrary our whole lives does not mean that it's true. The devil's most common method of trickery is implementing into our minds a false sense of salvation; to dupe us into believing that we don't have to take certain steps in order to inherit eternal life. Satan will do whatever he can to make an *absolute principle* of Christianity seem insignificant. This present life has been given to us so that we may continually seek God further and find out these truths for ourselves. First and foremost, we must understand the primary steps toward salvation (the principles) in order to move forward:

> Therefore leaving the principles of the doctrine of Christ, let us go on unto perfection; not laying again the foundation of <u>repentance</u> from dead works, and of faith toward God, Of <u>the doctrine of baptisms</u>, . . .
> —Hebrews 6:1-2

The passage above, which focuses on the "principles" of Christianity, specifically lists *Repentance* and the doctrine of *Baptisms*, which covers *water* baptism and the baptism of the *Holy Spirit*. Again, not one step is more important than the other (I John 5:8). That is why we cannot preach that one step (repentance) is a requirement while the other two steps (baptism & Holy Ghost) are optional. We must preach nothing short of what the apostles repeatedly confirmed: the three-fold cord of *Death, Burial,* and *Resurrection* (I Cor 15:3-4); which is our *Repentance, Baptism, and Holy Ghost infilling* (Acts 2:38); and thusly symbolizes the *Blood, Water, and Spirit* (I John 5:7)! These three things are very powerful because they work together to *ignite* our salvation; thusly forming a threefold cord which is not quickly broken (Eccl 4:12). Now and henceforth, whenever someone asks, *"What must I do to be saved"* we cannot afford to neglect the answer that was first given:

> . . . Repent, and be baptized <u>every one of you</u> in the name of Jesus Christ for the remission of sins, and ye shall receive the gift of the Holy Ghost.
> —Acts 2:38

Author's Note: The purpose of this book is NOT to point out the shortcomings of others; it is to paint a clearer picture of what the apostles actually believed and taught so that we may apply these principles to ourselves. John Phillips, author of the book *Exploring Hebrews* states: *"The Old Testament Israelites believed in God to bring them out of Egypt, but they did not believe in God to bring them into Cannan. The Israelites were content with half a salvation, . . . and that is all they received. Those who disbelieved had to be content with a second-class life in the wilderness, and there they died, never enjoying the rest of Cannan."*

Overall we must understand what separates certain teachings from others. When it comes to the Plan of Salvation just know that modifying God's plan—or teaching that certain steps are nonessential or optional—is an abomination. Altering Gods covenants is more or less a manner of ruling out God's plan (Mk 7:13). The following sections are probably as specific as this book gets whereas these chapters reveal the most prominent man-made traditions among the denominational churches.

Each of the following two chapters become even more eye-opening when compared to the other, whereas the traditions in which each chapter addresses intertwines with the other. And as you will see by reading the remainder of the book this combination of doctrines has become the most prominent view of the Christian faith over the past seventeen-hundred years—though it was not what was first spoken by the Lord or confirmed by the apostles nearly two-thousand years ago.

4

Itching Ears' Preferred Tradition

How shall we escape, if we neglect so great salvation;
which . . . <u>was confirmed unto us by them that heard him</u>;
—Hebrews 2:3

D uring a discussion with a member of a local
nondenominational church I was asked a very
contemplative question: *"Why do you trust the apostles
so much and rely on everything they did when Jesus is our example?"*
Well, good question. While the simple answer is *"because the
teachings of Jesus were written about by the apostles"* there is more
to it than just that. For now just realize that if we can't rely on
the men who wrote the Bible then we cannot rely on the words
of Jesus Himself, whereas His words *are* their words (for the most
part). And even though the most *important* answer to his question
should have been disclosed by reading the passage above, I believe
that, sadly, Hebrews 2:3 may not be enough to convince even
Christians that a mere *form* of Christianity will never measure up
to the actual foundation laid by the apostles in the Book of Acts.

Referring to my discussion with this church member; this was
actually a scheduled meeting set up for the purpose of discussing
our understanding of the Gospel. However, my personal intentions
were to discuss the differences between *man-made traditions* and
apostolic truths which often go unnoticed. I wanted to talk about

specific matters commonly overlooked; real-life doctrines which are typically ignored; Truths in which Satan would twist in order to "deceive the very elect" (Matt 24:24). More specifically—and while many consider this to be trivial—my questions concentrated on the reason why the apostles obeyed the Great Commission (in every account) by specifically declaring the actual name of Jesus Christ rather than repeating the phrase, *"Father, Son, Holy Spirit"* (as seen in Matthew 28:19). Even though I verified in Scripture exactly how the early church members specifically carried out the command of baptism, the issue seemed to be of little concern to those I met with. As you will see by reading the following sections this matter absolutely deserves a great deal of attention whereas it revolves around one of God's covenants—that, and the fact that Matthew 28:19 in particular is thought by many Bible scholars, theologians and historians to have been the victim of Biblical interpolation (a textual alteration made by early Catholic scribes).

Nevertheless—and as I previously stated—Satan will do his best to veil Truth from the world by having us believe that some of the more urgent matters are only of little importance (II Cor 4:3-4). As this book was written for the purpose of understanding the minds of the apostles more accurately, for that very reason we must understand *why* we should trust these men; *why* the churches of today should be functioning the same way as the early church. Furthermore, the early church—being the very, very first church in the world—is more or less the pattern for what today's churches should be. If everyone *truly* observed which doctrines *were* and were *not* being taught by the apostle's then nobody would rightly be able to say,

"That's just your interpretation of Scripture. I perceive the Word of God a little differently . . . so let's just agree to disagree."

Frankly, if a saint made a comment like this in the early church they would have been rebuked. Sadly it seems as though statements like this are more accepted these days than those which actually contend for the Truth. Still, the apostles, who believed in only

ONE true church body and ONE belief system (Eph 4:4-5), were in agreement about the doctrines in which they stood so firm. They did not "agree to disagree." They exhorted to one another that . . .

> . . . ye should earnestly contend for the faith which was once delivered unto the saints.
> —Jude 3

> . . . that ye all speak the same thing, and that there be no divisions among you; but that ye be perfectly joined together in the same mind and in the same judgment.
> —I Corinthians 1:10

> Preach the word; be instant in season, out of season; reprove, rebuke, exhort with all longsuffering and doctrine.
> —II Timothy 4:2

Inarguably, the Bible teaches that different views, interpretations, and opinions of Scripture are unacceptable to God (Deut 12:32, Prov 30:6, Luke 11:17, I Cor 1:10, Eph 4:4-5, II Tim 2:15, 3:16, II Peter 3:16, etc). As I mentioned in the introduction, the Christian faith more or less publicizes its hypocrisy simply because the thousands of denominations all over the world make it evident. When people *"agree to disagree,"* it goes against one of the chief principles of Christianity, which is unity. Obviously the New Testament was not intended for us to disagree with one another or to eventually bring different ideas and opinions into the Christian faith. These letters and treatises were meant for us to be in agreement with one another and to follow these patterns ourselves.

---

†

During a meeting in which I spoke about following in the apostles' footsteps and how we as "Christians" have failed to uphold this principle, a listener asked, *"If we should follow the Apostle Paul's example then should we follow him in his mistakes?"*

Out of many questions I've been asked regarding my faith this question was definitely the least reflective whereas it was more or less the product of sarcasm and close-mindedness; and yes, someone actually did ask me this. Yet I must say that our attitudes should not be cynical when we are faced with such reasonable inquiries. The Bible teaches us to be *quick to listen, slow to speak, and slow to wrath* (James 1:19). Furthermore—referring to his question—the Apostle Paul did not say, *"Follow my example as I make mistakes."* His statement was,

> Be ye followers of me, <u>even as I also am of Christ</u> . . . . remember me in all things, and keep the ordinances, as I delivered them to you.
> —I Corinthians 11:1-2

Of course we must follow Christ's example. Nonetheless, because Jesus was not physically (bodily) present during the establishment of the church, He left this responsibility in the hands of certain individuals; His disciples, the *apostles*, the *elect*, the *called*, the *chosen*, His *witnesses*, His *messengers;* some as teachers, some as pastors, some as prophets, and some as evangelists (I Cor 12:28, Eph 4:11-12). Notice what Jesus imparts to His disciples just before He left them to go back to Jerusalem to launch the church:

> . . . *and ye shall be witnesses unto me both in Jerusalem, and in all Judaea, and in Samaria, and unto the uttermost part of the earth.*
> —Acts 1:8

Concerning Paul specifically; Ananias was instructed by the Lord to meet up with the Apostle Paul (or Saul of Tarsus at the time), though Ananias was skeptical of the whole state of affairs whereas Saul's reputation classified him under the "Christian-killer" category. Even so, the Lord said unto him,

> . . . *Go thy way: for he* [Paul] *is a chosen vessel unto me,*
> *to bear my name before the Gentiles, and kings, and the*
> *children of Israel:*
>
> —Acts 9:15

Many are able to accept that the New Testament is "God-breathed," believing that the apostles were correct in everything they wrote. Yet when it comes down to addressing specific—sometimes controversial—issues like *baptism modes, the trinity doctrine vs. the Oneness of God,* and *the Pentecostal experience* (which is the infilling of the Holy Ghost *with the evidence* of speaking in tongues), many churches today believe their own methods, doctrines, and traditions (even personal opinions) have more authority over the original apostolic doctrines. And even though this may *seem* unreasonable we must ask ourselves the following questions (regarding these same issues) in order to set things further into perspective—that, and to reveal the main topics in which the remainder of this book offers:

➤ Did any of the apostles *clearly* write about or *plainly* teach that the Godhead is divided into three "persons" or "members"? Answer: NO; so *when* did this philosophy originate, *who* introduced it, and *why* is it so accepted as the only true depiction of God? Furthermore, what did these men really believe about the Godhead? What did they actually document?

➤ Did the apostles ever baptize anyone by repeating the titles *Father, Son, Holy Spirit?* Answer: NO; so *when* did this tradition begin, *who* introduced it, and *why* is it accepted more widely than the apostles' mode of baptism (in Jesus' name)?

While these issues may *seem* inconsequential we must realize that, because it involves knowing the identity of God and understanding His ordinances and promises (II Peter 3:9), these issues cannot be brushed aside or denoted as "useless controversies" (Titus 3:9). Additionally we cannot afford to allow our personal opinions determine what we believe before investigating the facts of the matter. Frankly, because certain doctrines either *were* or were *not* discussed amongst the early church; for that reason we must *"study to show ourselves approved"* all the more. Some things *were* taught by the apostles, and some things were *not*. And when considering the topics above in connection with the contemporary churches of today there are a few sobering *realities* involved:

➤ The *Sad Reality* is that the *majority* of today's contemporary churches do not uphold the apostles' doctrine on these specific matters.

➤ The *Tragic Reality* is that by not keeping these doctrines (*as they were taught* by the apostles) it can have an effect on our salvation. In other words, if we are not *"contending for the faith that was once delivered unto the saints"* (Jude 3)—if we do not keep the Gospel as it was taught by these men—then, according to the Bible, our belief is in vain (I Cor 15:2).

When it comes down to certain teachings of the apostles we must again realize that Jesus was not physically with these men during their ministry. Therefore, we must observe how the *apostles* operated the church. More specifically and for my first example, Jesus Christ did not baptize anyone during His ministry on earth; only the disciples did:

. . . Jesus made and baptized more disciples than John,
(Though Jesus himself baptized not, but his disciples,)
—John 4:1-2

For that reason we must observe exactly how the apostles carried out this act, examine the words which they spoke, and learn why they fulfilled the command so specifically.

Furthermore, during His ministry on earth Jesus did not lay his hands on anyone for the purpose of filling them with the Holy Ghost. Yet He did speak the following words:

> *Verily, verily, I say unto you, He that believeth on me, the works that I do shall he do also; <u>and greater works than these shall he do</u>; . . .*
>
> —John 14:12

One of the "greater works" that we see from the apostles in the Book of Acts, for instance, is the laying on of hands to fill others with the Holy Spirit. The fact is that even though the apostles laid a solid foundation involving specific doctrines, customs, methods, and other truths, what itching ears don't want to hear is that the majority today is guilty of the following:

➤ SELECTIVE ACCEPTANCE: Many *claim* to believe that every portion of the Bible is true and that we are required to preach what is written in it. Yet these same people cannot accept that some of the things they personally believe are actually extra-Biblical teachings; alternative explanations or opinions of the Bible that were introduced to the church years *after* the deaths of the apostles; selectively accepting—or disregarding rather—anything which may not agree with what he or she may have been taught by man in seminary school.

➤ SELECTIVE OBEDIENCE: Many assume that certain models or instructions throughout the epistles do not pertain to—or are *not* required of—us today because of how long ago these letters were written (thusly making portions of God's Word obsolete altogether by adding only a *limited* amount of God's Word to ourselves). Many believe we do not need to uphold certain customs in order to be labeled as Christians; selectively obeying the commands of God by neglecting certain instructions in the epistles, claiming that *"these things only applied to the early church."*

A major factor in understanding why we should trust the apostles is that the four Gospels—*including the words of Jesus*—were authored by these men. While this may be common sense to many it is the *gravity* of the circumstance that is typically unappreciated. Even though Jesus is the Man who *spoke* the *"red letters"* He is not the person who *wrote* them. While many have it in their minds to refer only to what Jesus Himself said we must realize that what is written in *red* is actually—for the most part—what *the apostles* remembered Him saying. Therefore, whether you are reading words that appear in *red* or **black**—in other words, whether you are reading the words of Christ or the apostles' commentary—ultimately *most* of what we read is what came from the thoughts and memories of the apostles (aside from certain alterations and insertions made by early scribes). Moreover, if *"ALL Scripture is given by inspiration of God and is profitable for doctrine and correction"* (II Tim 3:16) then we must realize that what is written in **black** has just as much authority as what is written in *red*. Again . . .

> . . . acknowledge that the things I write unto you are
> the commandments of the Lord.
>   —I Corinthians 14:37

Seeing how the passage above was written by the Apostle Paul wouldn't you say that trusting his words and actions is absolutely imperative in attaining salvation? Absolutely! We mustn't underestimate the apostolic authority given to these men whereas they were:

➢ Chosen by God to be His witnesses to carry out His instructions and to show the world how to do the same
➢ They either knew God as a human (the disciples) or had a close and personal encounter with Him (Paul).
➢ Chosen by God to build and operate a functional and productive church
➢ They wrote the New Testament, which consists of instructions, standards and customs and also shows us exactly how they carried out the commands of Christ.

Everything we know and understand about the Lord was made possible because of these men. I would say that we are safe to put our confidence not only in Christ, but also in the apostles who provided us with the knowledge of Christ through their testimonies and writings. Furthermore, if Jesus Christ was able to put His confidence in the apostles—and since we are to "follow His example"—then shouldn't we put our confidence in these men as well? Observe the following passage as it entails a conversation between the high priest and Jesus Himself just hours before the crucifixion. Notice the response Jesus offers:

> The high priest then asked Jesus of his disciples, and of his doctrine. Jesus answered him, *I spake openly to the world;* . . . *Why askest thou me? ask them which heard me, what I have said unto them: behold, they know what I said.*
> —John 18:19-21

According to the passage above Jesus makes it very clear that we are to rely upon the testimonies of the men that heard Him. If people truly believe that we are to obey Jesus and *"only go by what HE said"* then we cannot neglect the fact that He said we must listen to the disciples' testimonies. If we neglect the words and actions of the apostles then ultimately we are disregarding the Lord Jesus Himself (I Thess 4:8).

The Interpretation

That ye may be mindful . . . of the commandment of us the apostles of the Lord and Saviour:
—II Peter 3:2

Now that we know we can trust the apostles let's observe the command known as The Great Commission, whereas this issue seems to hold much confusion among the denominational mainstream. As we previously discussed the apostles believed that baptism is a part of salvation (Mark 16:16, John 3:5); therefore, we must observe the specific mode in which the apostles actually used in order to determine the proper way to perform this ordinance of God ourselves. Not only that, we must be able to determine when and where other modes were formulated (and history *does* reveal these things). Because the Bible teaches that there is only ONE baptism (Eph 4:5) it is our obligation to uphold this one-and-only baptism. Additionally, we must be able to identify exactly what makes other modes of baptism illegitimate. Having said that, observe the Great Commission according to the Book of Matthew in our English Bibles:

> *Go ye therefore, and teach all nations, baptizing them in the name of the Father, and of the Son, and of the Holy Ghost:*
> —Matthew 28:19

Today in most denominational churches the most common mode of baptism is practiced by simply *repeating* the words from the passage above. The typical way of thinking is that, because Matthew 28:19 illustrates these as the words of Jesus then we must simply repeat what is written here rather than to observe how the apostles obeyed the command themselves. Remember, the Bible says that what Jesus first spoke was *confirmed* by the men that heard Him (Heb 2:3); therefore, we must observe the *only* way in which the command was actually obeyed. Furthermore—even though it is highly debated among Bible scholars and historians whether the phrase *"Father, Son, Holy Ghost"* even existed in the original manuscripts of Matthew—we are still able to detect the only method in which the apostle's practiced. Remember, Jesus Himself did not baptize (John 4:2); only his disciples did. Now, observe the following verse. Here is the interpretation and confirmation of the command from Peter's perspective as he attempts to fulfill the Great Commission for the first time in history:

> . . . Repent, and be baptized every one of you <u>in the name of Jesus Christ</u> for the remission of sins, . . .
> —Acts 2:38

Now, I realize that many readers have probably never heard the difference between Matthew 28:19 and Acts 2:38 (baptism in the titles vs. Jesus Name Baptism) so let me break it down:

> ➤ In our modern English Bibles today Matthew 28:19 offers a *command*, which Jesus presented to the disciples: Acts 2:38 is the *same* command being carried out (interpreted and obeyed) by the men who heard Jesus.
> ➤ One verse teaches what may have been *spoken* by the Lord, but the other verse is what was *confirmed* by the Apostle Peter.
> ➤ One verse tells us WHAT to do; the other verse teaches us HOW to do it.

We cannot observe one verse without referring to the other; otherwise we would be taking Scripture out of the context in which it was written. (When Matthew 28:19 is repeated as a baptismal formula it is, no doubt, being taken out of its context.) Even though there are diverse modes and formulas of baptism practiced by today's churches, the New Testament writings conclude that the apostles practiced only ONE baptism, thusly submitting to Ephesians 4:5, which plainly teaches that there is only *"one baptism."* Not to say that any person is "wrong" for undergoing the triune baptism in the titles (if that is all they are familiar with and are serving God in all sincerity); maybe just "partially correct" for not fully comprehending the command the same way as the disciples. Nonetheless, it is crucial that we first understand the *purpose* for the mode of baptism in which we follow, whether it is repeating Matthew 28:19 or continuing and upholding the apostle's method—specifically declaring His *Name*. There is no way to fully understand the actual command itself (in Matthew 28:19) without observing the confirming action (in Acts 2:38).

I have heard many people defend their faith by stating, *"Acts 2:38 was just Peter's words, and I want to go by what Jesus said."* However, that is a very dangerous way of thinking. I even heard one person ask: *"Who are you gonna trust, Jesus or Peter?"*

Unfortunately these mentalities only suggest that Peter did NOT comprehend the Lords command—that he did not have an accurate understanding of the will of God. In effect, we shouldn't think that we have a better understanding of this command than the men (witnesses) who actually traveled, abided, ate, and learned from Jesus Himself. Make sense? Furthermore, if we cannot rely on the men that heard Jesus then I guess we cannot rely on the following fulfillments and interpretations of the command, which further support Peter's interpretation. The following passages illustrate the ONLY baptism mode in which the early New Testament church knew of and practiced:

- But when they believed Philip preaching the things concerning the kingdom of God, and the name of Jesus Christ, they were baptized, . . .

  —Acts 8:12

- . . . only they were baptized in the name of the Lord Jesus.

  —Acts 8:16

- And he commanded them to be baptized in the name of the Lord.

  —Acts 10:48

- . . . they were baptized in the name of the Lord Jesus.

  —Acts 19:5

- . . . be baptized, . . . calling on the name of the Lord.

  —Acts 22:16

- . . . but ye are washed, but ye are sanctified, but ye are justified in the name of the Lord Jesus,

  —I Corinthians 6:11

The passages above only verify that Peter's interpretation of the Great Commission was more about affirming the actual NAME of Jesus rather than to merely repeat the titles *Father, Son, Holy Ghost*. One thing to keep in mind is that if Satan is going to take the time to misconstrue the Word of God he would start by attacking the actual words of Christ rather than the confirming words of the apostles (which appear quite repeatedly). What I mean is that, while the phrase "Father, Son, Holy Ghost" appears only once in the Bible, we are more apt to focus more on this verse because it bids Jesus' words, thusly ignoring the *recurrent* examples of the apostles' confirmations. However, if we are so caught up on observing the words of Christ to the point that we deemphasize other passages—even ignoring or denying the apostles' words—then we become guilty of picking-and-choosing a salvation plan of our own. Yet because ALL Scripture is given for *doctrine* and *correction* (II Tim 3:16)—and because the majority is so determined to focus on the words of Jesus only—then we cannot neglect the following passage, which also imparts the words of Jesus Himself and further substantiates the apostles' confirmation:

> *Thus it is written, . . . that repentance and <u>remission of sins should be preached in his name</u> among all nations, beginning at Jerusalem.*
> —Luke 24:46-47

When comparing Acts 2:38 to the passage above it should be very eye-opening to see just how accurately Peter's actions fulfilled Jesus' words. We see that not only did Jesus predict WHAT would happen, WHERE it would take place, and WHO all would be present; He also foretold HOW it would be accomplished (in His Name); by whose authority it would be fulfilled. Subsequently, we see that Peters words (Acts 2:38) undeniably fulfilled the words of Christ. That is why Jesus continued His impartation with these following words:

> *And ye are witnesses of these things.*
> —Luke 24:48

Were the disciples wrong for not repeating the titles *Father, Son, Holy Ghost,* or did they simply understand that there was a specific way to obey the Lord's command? Wouldn't the most reasonable assumption be that these men, who were more qualified to interpret the command than anyone, simply understand that the NAME of the Father, the Son, and the Holy Spirit is Jesus Christ? Absolutely! The Bible even states just prior to what Jesus affirmed in the passages above that He opened up the disciples understanding (Luke 24:45). In other words, they were not in the dark about what they were commissioned to do. Considering that, let's observe some other words spoken by the Lord so that we may be able to better comprehend exactly what the apostles understood. Observe Christ's prayer:

> I have manifested _thy name_ unto the men which thou gavest me out of the world: . . . And I have declared unto them _thy name_, and will declare it:
> —John 17:6, 26

Considering the passage above in addition with the words and actions of the apostles—by this I mean rightly dividing the testaments in which the apostles-themselves wrote—we are able to substantially conclude that the apostles understood the following:

➢ The NAME of the Father is Jesus (John 5:43; 17:6, 26). Jesus is the Father
➢ The NAME of the Son is Jesus (Luke 1:31, etc). Jesus is the Son
➢ The NAME of the Holy Ghost is Jesus (John 14:26). Jesus is the Holy Ghost

The Bible is very clear. The disciples were not confused about their expectations; nor were they confused about the _name_ of God. The Jehovah of the Old Testament appeared to the world as Jesus Christ of the New Testament (John 10:30; 12:45; 14:9). Knowing this they also understood that He is referred to by many titles, they were aware that the "name" (singular) of the Father, Son, and Holy Ghost (Matt 28:19) is Jesus Christ (Acts 2:38). As a matter of fact they understood that believing on His NAME is a commandment:

> And this is his commandment, That we should believe on the name of his Son Jesus Christ, . . .
> —I John 3:23

Additionally, the apostles believed that no other NAME will save us:

> Be it known unto you all, . . . that by the name of Jesus Christ . . . which has become the head of the corner. Neither is there salvation in any other: <u>for there is none other name under heaven given among men, whereby we must be saved</u>.
> —Acts 4:10-12

The apostles believed that every *word* and *action* was to be said and done in the NAME of the Lord Jesus Christ, whether it was praying, healing, casting out demons—even baptizing:

> And <u>whatsoever ye do</u> in word or deed, <u>do all in the name of the Lord Jesus</u>, giving thanks to God and the Father by him.
> —Colossians 3:17

Basically, the most important thing to understand about the Great Commission is that Jesus never intended for the church to eliminate His name and repeat a mere phrase. His desire—according to the apostles—is that we acknowledge His name (Luke 24:47). If the command were intended to be carried out by simply repeating the phrase then the apostles would have *known* to do this, they would have *carried out* the command this way themselves, and they would have *included* this specification somewhere in their writings. As strict as these men were, it would have been made known to the world through Scripture that we must repeat the titles rather than upholding the Name. Again, this is more than just a mere *useless controversy*; it is a matter of altering a covenant between God and man. More specifically, in this case it is either a matter of *forsaking* the name of the Lord or *upholding* it.

❖ The Network:

> *I know thy works: . . . for thou hast a little strength, and hast kept my word, and hast not denied my name.*
> —Revelation 3:8

Overall, we must observe more carefully how the apostles operated the early church (Rom 16:17, II Tim 3:14). If we neglect to observe and follow the commands the same way as the apostles then we are ignoring the very men God chose as His witnesses; thusly, ignoring God Himself (I Thess 4:8). *If we believe man-made traditions—though inconsistent with the apostle's—are acceptable to God then we are forced to believe also that there are teachings in the world with greater authority than the original apostolic foundation.* Regarding those who exhort the method of repeating Matthew 28:19 (I'll just be straight forward): considering the fact that Scripture clearly teaches that the apostle's believed in Jesus-Name-Baptism; if you have not taken the time to understand *why* the apostles never settled for repeating a passage that didn't yet exist then it's *possible* that you haven't searched for God with all your hearts (Jer 29:13). Nevertheless, if you have endured this challenge up to now then I must say that you are definitely seeking, and I commend you for that. Nevertheless, we must understand where, when, and why the church began to practice alternative formulas. Remember, history was written for our insight (Rom 15:4).

Most people who believe in repeating the titles do not even know when this tradition originated or even the name of the person that first presented this idea. It is most presumptuously concluded that because Matthew 28:19 states in red letters *"Father, Son, Holy Ghost,"* . . . we are supposed to *"say what Jesus said"* instead of observing the apostles' confirming actions. In truth, if we just took the time to understand the mode of baptism in which we choose to follow instead of accepting that which we are accustomed to then we might be able to see how the principle of *research* (Rom 15:4, II Tim 2:15, I Pet 3:15) may enlighten us in other areas as well. As the following section affirms, investigation makes all the difference in understanding Truth. Now, if you DO believe in repeating the titles instead of speaking the name; please continue to read while I fill you in on *WHY* you believe *WHAT* you believe.

The New Tradition

> . . . but there be some that trouble you, and would pervert the gospel of Christ.
>
> —Galatians 1:7

You now know—because we just covered it—that NONE of the apostles repeated the title-phrase as seen in Matthew. During the first century before the book of Matthew had even been written the apostles believed the titles *Father, Son, & Holy Spirit* (Counselor) applied to only ONE divine being; that is, GOD, the Creator of the universe (Notice that Matthew 28:19 even uses the singular word *"name"* rather than the plural form *"names"*). The apostles did not believe these titles referred to three limited or distinct persons among the Godhead. They were familiar with the prophecy of Isaiah, which depicts God the Father, Jesus the man, and the Holy Spirit as ONE and the same:

> For unto us a child is born, . . . a son is given: . . . his name shall be called . . . Counselor, The mighty God, The everlasting Father, The Prince of Peace.
>
> —Isaiah 9:6

God, who is ONE Lord (Deut 6:4), is referred to by many titles, each depicting the various offices and roles in which He chooses to manifest Himself to mankind. The apostles believed God is an unlimited Spirit, who is able to not only manifest Himself in the physical world while maintaining His omnipresence in the spiritual realm but also who is able to do so without being multiple *"persons"* or *"members"* (there will be Scripture for these things in the following chapter).

I remember hearing a very insightful and fundamental statement about the three most recognized manifestations of God: *"He is our Father through His relationship with us, Son by His physical incarnation and sacrificial purpose, and Holy Ghost in action and instruction; yet He is only One Spirit"* (John 4:24, I Cor 12:11, Eph 4:4). The apostles did not believe in the philosophy of the trinity because this idea had not yet been presented to the world. As a matter of fact, Bible scholars and historians would agree that the trinity doctrine did not enter the church until nearly two centuries after Christ's ministry on earth. The TRUTH is that when the trinity doctrine *first* began to surface among the churches it was not accepted because to them trinitarianism was no different from tritheism. Notice Peter's warning:

> . . . there shall be false teachers among you, who privily shall bring in damnable heresies, even denying the Lord that bought them, . . . many shall follow their pernicious ways; by reason of whom the way of truth shall be evil spoken of.
>
> —II Peter 2:1-2

Not only does Peter state that false teachers would be among the church, he also predicts that many would reject the Truth and follow these false teachers. The early churches definitely considered this to be a reality, and many were slain for contending for the faith in which the original apostles first proclaimed. That's right! Once the philosophy of the trinity began to be widespread many true saints were killed for rejecting it. Yet these saints were only doing as they were instructed and were rejecting new doctrines (Col 2:8-9, II John 1:10, etc). Ironically, many today—because of the trinitarian philosophy which has been passed down over the centuries—have simply accepted that *"God is three persons"* and that *"it is a mystery in which the human mind cannot fully comprehend"* rather than doing the research and uncovering these truths ourselves.

Conversely, *the apostles*—rather than believing in a distinction of actual "persons" among the Godhead—believed there was only a distinction between His flesh and Spirit. God illustrates various manifestations in both the physical world and spiritual realm, He reveals numerous aspects of His nature and offers many titles to represent His many characteristics; yet He gave only one NAME through which salvation can be attained (Acts 4:10-12). These are just a few reasons why the Bible shows absolutely NO account of baptism being performed by repeating the titles. Frankly, these triune philosophies had not yet been presented to the world. (Again, the following chapter will cover the trinity doctrine in more depth.) Nonetheless, because the trinitarian philosophy plays a major role in understanding the current topic under discussion (baptism), for now I will only impart that it was not a part of the original Gospel Message. None of the apostles believed in it, nor did they baptize using the phrase *"Father, Son, Holy Spirit."* These two doctrines were cleverly intertwined and were sanctioned in the fourth century by the Roman government as the only accepted (legal) form of Christianity (see ch. 6).

As I previously mentioned it is highly debated among Bible scholars—and *many* other sources attest—that the phrase *"Father, Son, Holy Ghost"* was not included in any Greek manuscript prior to the fourth century. While there are tangible reasons as to *why,* the most prominent conclusions lie in the fact that there are absolutely NO other included texts in the New Testament wording this phrase at it is seen in Matthew. In fact, no other book in the New Testament includes these titles in the same sentence even. In contrast, however, it was common for Jesus to use the phrase *"In My name"* whereas we find seventeen occurrences of this throughout the Gospels (Matt 18:5,20; 24:5, Mark 9:37,39,41; 13:6; 16:17, Luke 9:48; 21:8, John 14:13,14,26; 15:16; 16:23,24,26). This further illustrates why there is not one event recorded in the New Testament where the apostles used the title-phrase as seen in the book of Matthew.

The reality is that, according to many encyclopedic references (listed in the back), the phrase *"Father, Son, Holy Ghost"* is believed to have not been included in the original manuscript of Matthew's Gospel. Substantial allegations conclude that the Apostle Matthew did not write this passage originally. The Catholic Church merely borrowed Justin Martyr's baptismal formula and changed the text of Matthew 28:19. Strong evidence points to the fact that Matthew 28:19—as we see it in our English Bibles—was actually a late liturgical insertion; an addition. (Again, for more confirmation see the section in the back titled, *"Matthew 28:19 . . . Forged?"*)

❖ The Network:

> As also in all his epistles, speaking in them of these things; in which are some things hard to be understood, which they that are unlearned and unstable wrest, as they do also the other scriptures, unto their own destruction.
>
> —II Peter 3:16

One version of the Bible uses the phrase *"twisting the Scriptures."* Man has been distorting the Word of God—even adding to it—ever since it was first spoken and twisting Scripture ever since it was first written. When Matthew wrote his Gospel account in roughly 70 AD, only then should we consider his Gospel to be without error. Over the course of time through the progressive translation process the fallibility tends to increase due to human error—that and textual insertions in which the powers of this dark world may implement. During the first few centuries when false teaching flourished among the land it was a reality for scribes to alter Scriptural text. As a matter of fact, the testimony of *Eusebius*, a Bishop of Caesarea and early Christian writer (265AD-339AD) attests to quite the opposite of what modern tradition offers.

Being a man of high clerical status and considered to be the most educated man of his era, Eusebius was permitted to view the early New Testament writings held in the Library of Caesarea. He testifies in his *Proof of the Gospel, Book III Ch 7, 136 (a-d), p. 157* that the original manuscript of Matthew's Gospel bids Jesus' original words as, *"Go, and make disciples of all the nations in my Name."* In fact, Eusebius believed the textual alteration that we see today in our English Bibles was the most severe of any falsification to the Gospel and he denounced its addition to the modern texts. Unfortunately, because the Catholic Church destroyed (burned) every copy of the N.T. manuscripts dating prior to the fourth century, we have no original (unaltered) copies in existence to this day. The only testament we are able to research is what Eusebius has supplied us with through his writings.

❖ The Network:

> For there is nothing covered, that shall not be revealed; neither hid, that shall not be known. Therefore whatsoever ye have spoken in darkness shall be heard in the light;
> —Luke 12:2-3

Even though the majority of Christians will never consider the progressive translation process and will simply assume that the Bible contains absolutely no errors, the truth is that there is a difference between the following:

➤ The *infallible* (perfect) Word of God: this was *spoken* by the Lord
➤ The original, *inerrant* (dependable) New Testament manuscripts: these were *written* by the apostles
➤ Our modern Bibles: a process of many phases; translated, modified, altered and duplicated by men (containing some deliberate alterations but many spelling and punctuation errors)

Though Matthew 28:19 may appear in our English Bible versions, the idea of baptizing in the titles *Father, Son, Holy Ghost* was first introduced by a man named *Justin Martyr,* whose outlook on religion was quite universalistic. He actually could not differentiate the God of Abraham from the god of Plato. And because Greek philosophy was so influential in his life, Martyr decided by his own authority to combine pagan practice with Christian ordinances. More specifically, he altered the mode of baptism—not by changing the text of Scripture but by practicing a different verbal formula. Instead of continuing in the apostles' doctrine (proclaiming Jesus' actual name) Martyr's innovation was to simply speak the words, *"Father, Son, Holy Ghost."* Consequently, his formula influenced many other apologists of his time and was eventually sanctioned by the Catholic Church as the only legal mode of baptism. *In fact, the Catholic Encyclopedia II, pg 263 even admits to changing the baptismal formula from the name of Jesus Christ to "Father, Son, Holy Spirit."*

When considering everything above it becomes quite peculiar that there is only one verse in our modern Bibles that contains the phrase *"Father, Son, Holy Ghost."* But since Matthew 28:19 is the only verse in which the majority focuses on and considers to be the most reputable then shouldn't we expect to find at least one other passage worded the same way? One would assume. Still, because the book of Matthew hadn't yet been written during the early apostolic era (until roughly 70 AD)—whether it contained the title-phrase or not—nobody could have possibly thought to simply repeat the Great Commission as it is worded in his Gospel (given that it is *not* an alteration).

However, because these waters can be very dangerous to tread (so I've been told), let's focus more on what applies to us today. Since our modern Bibles actually *do* include the phrase *"Father, Son, Holy Ghost"* we more than likely consider this verse to be just as authoritative as any of Jesus' words, though it is possible they are not. Nonetheless, here's the kicker: *Whether it is an alteration or not, the fact is that Matthew 28:19 still teaches that baptism must be practiced by applying "the Name."* Furthermore, because Jesus-Name-Baptism was the method practiced during the early apostolic era and is what was bound in Heaven (Matt 16:18-19) we must hold fast to this doctrine as it was taught:

> Holding fast the faithful word <u>as he hath been taught</u>,
> that he may be able by sound doctrine both to exhort
> <u>and convince the gainsayers</u>.
>
> —Titus 1:9

And convince the gainsayers? Wow! It seems that Paul also dealt with those having itching ears during his ministry. Perhaps this was the motive of his forewarning to Timothy (II Tim 4:3-4). Notice another piece of advice he imparts:

> But continue thou in the things which thou hast learned
> and hast been assured of, <u>knowing of whom thou hast
> learned them</u>;
>
> —II Timothy 3:14

While the church is—according to both passages above—instructed to continue in the things which were taught by the apostles, we are also expected to know *who* presented certain ideas to the world. And when considering Justin Martyr's formula; this was obviously a new teaching and a totally different theology. In other words, it is NOT the apostles' doctrine; it is a man-made tradition influenced by world religion. The following passage is one we have examined more than once already and one that we will examine again. However, when viewing this now it should become even more eye-opening:

> . . . *Howbeit in vain do they worship me, teaching for*
> *doctrines the commandments of men. For laying aside the*
> *commandment of God, ye hold the tradition of men, . . .*
> *Full well ye reject the commandment of God, that ye may*
> *keep your own tradition. Making the word of God of none*
> *effect through your tradition, which ye have delivered:*
> —Mark 7:7-9, 13

By holding to the tradition of *repeating* the titles many have rejected the commandment of God by not continuing in the apostle's footsteps. That is why it is a matter of concern; we were never supposed to accept the doctrine of triune baptism in the first place:

> If there come any unto you, <u>and bring not this doctrine</u>, receive him not into your house, neither bid him God speed:
>
> —II John 1:10

As for the early church it seems quite peculiar that we do not find mention in Scripture (or any other historical indication) that the topic of *"baptism modes"* was considered to be a controversial subject during this time. Rather it was common sense that baptism was to be practiced in Jesus' name. Nobody was confused or argued about the way baptism needed to be carried out. In fact, this is something that could *not* have been argumentative unless of course there was nothing to argue about in the first place. More specifically, if Eusebius' testimony is true—if Matthew 28:19 does not offer the true words of Christ—then it would only make sense why this confusion is not mentioned in the book of Acts or the epistles. It seems quite odd, unless these were not Jesus' original words and the phrase *"Father, Son, Holy Ghost"* didn't even exist during the time of the apostles' ministry (because it hadn't yet been thought of, until nearly a century later). The more logical conclusion would be that the actual events which took place happened *this* way and in *this* order (dates approx):

➢ Christ commissions the disciples to go make disciples of all nations while using the phrase *"In My name"* (30 AD)
➢ The Apostle Peter's confirmation of the covenant (30 AD)
➢ The New Testament church baptizes new converts in Jesus' name (30 AD-70 AD)
➢ Justin Martyr devises the new formula *"Father, Son, Holy Ghost"* (150 AD)

> ➤ The Catholic Church alters Matthew's Gospel to match Martyr's formula (300AD)
> ➤ Eusebius views the original, unaltered manuscripts of Matthew's Gospel and begins writing his own treatises (post-300 AD)
> ➤ The Catholic Church destroys every existing New Testament manuscript dating prior to the fourth century (325 AD)

One thing to keep in mind is that all of Eusebius' writings date prior to every New Testament manuscript in existence today! Considering the facts we have covered, the most logical conclusion would be that none of the apostles ever heard the phrase *"Father, Son, Holy Ghost"* proceed from the mouth of Christ.

Biblical or Extra-biblical?

For we write none other things unto you, than what ye read or acknowledge;

—II Corinthians 1:13

In view of everything we have covered up to this point is there any reason to believe that Martyr's modification was ever practiced by the apostles? Absolutely not! What many do not understand is the very thing this matter of concern revolves around: the difference between *Biblical* teachings and *extra-biblical* teachings.

> ➤ Biblical Teachings are doctrines taught by observing and relaying what Jesus and the apostles themselves taught.
> ➤ Extra-biblical Teachings are doctrines taught by using *portions* of Scripture (out of Biblical context), but were *not* actually taught by Jesus or the apostles.

For instance—and in regards to the issue at hand—while many today teach that baptism-in-the-titles is biblical because our Bibles show that Jesus worded His command this way, the Truth is that He did not teach anyone to merely *repeat* the phrase *"Father, Son, Holy Ghost."* Scripture teaches that baptism was instituted in every account by verbally proclaiming the actual name of the Lord Jesus Christ. Therefore [don't miss this] because the Bible teaches that there is only ONE BAPTISM (Eph 3:5) we must uphold this principle by determining which baptism is Biblical and which one is extra-biblical (which I believe we have already established). Allow me to further break it down:

> ➤ It is *Biblical* to teach that the apostles baptized in the name of the Lord Jesus Christ (Acts 2:38; 8:12; 8:16; 10:48; 19:5; 22:16, I Cor 6:11, and Gal 3:27).
> ➤ It is *extra-biblical* to teach that we are to simply repeat the phrase *"Father, Son, Holy Ghost,"* considering the fact that neither Jesus nor any of the apostles taught others to do so. Again, there is only . . .

> One Lord, one faith, <u>one baptism,</u>
> —Ephesians 4:5

Considering the fact that we have viewed *two* separate men with *two* different baptisms we must therefore come to a conclusion as to which baptism is approved of God and which one is not. One man was an apostle (Peter) while the other was merely a philosophical theist (Martyr). *Now, who was given the keys to the Kingdom of Heaven? Who did Jesus use to establish His covenant? Which baptism was bound in Heaven?* Remember:

> *And I say also unto thee, That thou art Peter, and upon this rock I will build my church; . . . And I will give unto thee the keys of the kingdom of heaven: and <u>whatsoever thou shalt bind on earth shall be bound in heaven</u>: . . .*
> —Matthew 16:18-19

Hopefully the passage above has filled in some of those gray areas. If you research the subject of *triune baptism* for yourself you will likely uncover the name *Tertullian*, which was the man responsible for introducing the triune-god theory. Tertullian adopted Martyrs baptism formula and combined it with his own teaching: *the trinity doctrine*. These two men were no more than vessels used to introduce these alterations to the Gospel. It wasn't until the year 325 AD that the Roman government sanctioned these "new theologies" as the only legal form of Christianity (aka, Roman Catholicism), which we will soon discuss. For now just know that during this era men were altering the Gospel like never before. The question to ask now would be: *Why was it during this era?* Why was the Gospel being attacked so severely and altered so drastically during *this* time in history? Good question. And this is HUGE! Basically, if these kinds of changes had been going on during the apostle's ministry, then nothing would have succeeded! So far we have observed just how strict the Apostle Paul was with the churches about even the slightest change or difference in doctrine. But here is where the rubber meets the road. Notice Paul's forewarning and farewell:

> For I know this, that after my departing shall grievous wolves enter in among you, not sparing the flock. Also of your own selves shall men arise, speaking perverse things, to draw away disciples after them. Therefore watch, and remember, that by the space of three years I ceased not to warn every one night and day with tears.
> —Acts 20:29-30

Paul knew—because he understood just how cunning the devil is—false teachers would enter the scene and attempt to deceive the world after he was out of the picture. And because Satan understood the importance of baptism he began his influence by altering the specific procedure which was bound in Heaven. Subsequently we see that it was only a span of a few decades after Paul's departing that these new traditions entered the world, whereas Martyr's modification to the baptismal formula took place around 150 AD.

Why this is important is because if we are practicing man-made traditions that have taken the place of the commands of God (Mark 7:7, 9, 13) then we are no better than the Pharisees. Bottom line: if we are currently teaching doctrines in which we do not know the origin then we are blind guides leading the blind.

> . . . And if the blind lead the blind, both shall fall into the ditch.
> —Matthew 15:14

Remission is in the Name

> *Thus it is written, . . . that repentance and <u>remission of sins should be preached in his name</u> among all nations, beginning at Jerusalem.*
> —Luke 24:46-47

When observing *specifically* what the Bible does and does not teach we are able to narrow down this matter to the following options:

> ➤ The Bible plainly teaches that baptism in the name of Jesus Christ will remit sins (Acts 2:38; 22:16).
> ➤ The Bible does NOT teach anywhere—nor did the apostles believe or even mention—that baptism in the titles *Father, Son, Holy Ghost* will remit sins.

Again, look very closely to what Acts 2:38 *specifically* states:

> . . . Repent, and be baptized every one of you <u>in the name of Jesus Christ for the remission of sins,</u> . . .
> —Acts 2:38

Nobody can deny that the Bible clearly says that *EVERYONE* must be baptized in the *NAME* of *JESUS CHRIST* in order to *REMIT* his or her *SINS*. This is why the Apostle Peter declared, *"there is none other name under Heaven given among men, whereby we must be saved"* (Acts 4:10-12). When someone believes sin can be remitted any other way than following this covenant of God then he or she believes something not written in the Bible; something that is in conflict with the passage above; something concluded by opinion. What it all boils down to is this: Either we DO agree with the apostles' baptism or we DON'T. If we do not agree then we must have solid Scripture to support and justify why the tradition of men has more authority over that which the apostles confirmed, bottom line!

One purpose of this book is to help people realize that we are expected to tell people WHY we believe WHAT we believe (I Peter 3:15). If we are unable to defend what we believe then we have failed to live up to our expectations as claimed Christians. Ultimately, if we are using different methods than the apostles then we are more or less saying that our man-made traditions have more authority over what is plainly written in the Bible. The only salvation plan bound in Heaven includes the specification of Jesus-Name-Baptism. The majority of today's churches overlook this detail because of what the naked eye has concluded from Matthew 28:19 (in addition with the traditions of men).

> But if our gospel be hid, it is hid to them that are lost:
> In whom the god of this world hath blinded the minds
> of them which believe not, . . .
>
> —II Corinthians 4:3-4

Tying It All Together

We have observed so far the only baptism method demonstrated by the early church; the only procedure offered in Scripture, that is. But before we venture into the next segment there is just one more thought, which is very relevant to what the remainder of this book offers. In Chapter One we discussed how the true body of Christ (or church) cannot be classified as a denomination or by the name on the church sign or billboard; it is the doctrine in which a person chooses to accept and obey that determines this. Additionally, we have covered some of the major differences between the early church and the churches of today. But here is where the rubber meets the road. As for those who feel as though the issue of denominationalism is irrelevant or that baptism is more of a *"personal conviction"* rather than an absolute requirement, please soak in the following thought: *Diverse modes of baptism is one of the determining factors and reveals what sets the one true church of God apart from mainstream Christianity.*

❖ The Network (read this carefully):

> Now I beseech you, brethren, by the name of our Lord Jesus Christ, that ye all speak the same thing, and that there be no divisions among you; but that ye be perfectly joined together in the same mind and in the same judgment. For it hath been declared unto me of you, . . . that there be contentions among you. Now this I say that every one of you saith, I am of Paul; and I of Apollos; and I of Cephas; and I of Christ. Is Christ divided? Was Paul crucified for you? Or were ye baptized in the name of Paul? I thank God that I baptized none of you, . . . Lest any man should say that I had baptized in mine own name.
>
> —I Corinthians 1:10-15

According to the passage above, the very issue of division (in this scenario) revolves around whose name they wanted to be identified with—even to the point that Paul clarifies which baptism they underwent. This is very noteworthy considering all we have discussed up to this point. It seems as though some of the different doctrines, which separate one church division from another, revolves around what people believe about water baptism. Some denote baptism as unnecessary, whereas others believe it is vital in attaining salvation (Mark 16:16). Some believe baptism is nothing more than a show of godliness (a public display), and others understand that it is a pledge of a clear conscience toward God (I Peter 3:21). Some lean to the notion that we must simply repeat the *red letters* from Matthew 28:19, while many uphold the *only* method used by the apostles (Acts 2:38). And finally, some consider this matter to be nothing more than a *"useless controversy"*, while the apostles believed baptism to be nothing less than a covenant between God and man (Matt 16:18-19, Mark 16:16, Luke 24:47, Acts 2:38).

Now, let's refer back to Chapter One to the theory which states that the *"one true church"* is a specific denomination which holds the name of Jesus. As I have stated already, the one true body of Christ cannot be classified or narrowed down to a denomination, whether it holds the name of Jesus or not. Actually, there *is* some truth to the "name-theory," but not in the essence as to the theory above. Moreover, it is *how* the name is applied to one's self. While anybody can put the name of the Lord Jesus Christ on their church building, unfortunately not everybody *applies* the name of Jesus in the same manner as the early church. The name of Jesus Christ must be applied to each *individual* through a very specific and symbolic procedure. Just for a moment consider what a groom expects from—or desires in—a woman before he takes her as his bride.

> ➤ He expects her to accept his proposal. This is her *pledge* to him.
> ➤ He expects her to be holy, undefiled, and unblemished.
> ➤ He expects her to take on his name.

Now consider some of what the apostles taught regarding water baptism, and notice the vast similarity between these examples:

> ➤ Baptism, the *pledge* toward God (I Peter 3:21)
> ➤ Preparation for the Bridegroom—we wash ourselves spotless as a pure, undefiled and unblemished bride for Him (Eph 5:25-27, see Rev 19:7)
> ➤ It is how we become united with and identified by Him; we take on His name in baptism (Gal 3:27)

> But these are written, that ye might believe that Jesus is
> the Christ, the Son of God; <u>and that believing ye might</u>
> <u>have life through his name</u>.
>
> —John 20:31

Much of what separates mainstream denominationalism from the true church body of Christ is *how* the name of Jesus is applied to each and every individual. If we want to *put on Christ though baptism* (Gal 3:27) then we must take on His name while doing so. This is what the apostles taught; it is what they believed! Overall, what classifies baptism-in-the-titles as an abomination—in addition to the fact that it excludes the name of the Lord Jesus Christ—is this: *tradition cannot take place of the original custom in which the apostles first mandated.* These men believed and taught that . . .

> . . . as many of you as have been baptized into Christ
> <u>have put on Christ</u>.
>
> —Galatians 3:27

In other words, we become *identified* by Christ or UNITED with Him. Depending on which mode of baptism a person undergoes determines WHO or WHAT he or she has been united with. *Ultimately* [and here's the severity of it all] *when a person has been baptized into the triune formula then he or she has been united with a mere tradition and not with Christ. It yokes a person with a man-made theology rather than an ordinance bound in Heaven.*

Obviously, when baptism-in-the-titles first became customary in the church the attitude among the post-apostolic church fathers was to *improve* the Gospel by introducing new theologies. In contrast, however, we should not think that the Gospel is something that can be improved by man. During this time—as people as people began to humanize the Gospel of Jesus Christ—what was actually happening was that people were no longer applying the name of Jesus Christ; they were applying a Catholic tradition in place of Gods ordinance. But again:

> *Full well ye reject the commandment of God, that ye may*
> *keep your own tradition. Making the word of God of none*
> *effect through your tradition, which ye have delivered:*
> —Mark 7:9, 13

In essence: the tradition of repeating the titles "Father, Son, Holy Ghost" has made the commandment of baptism of none effect. That's the abomination! There are many, who probably assume that—because you have been a "Christian" your whole life and have never been exposed to this—it does not apply to YOU. Nonetheless, (and referring to Acts 19 once again), the Apostle Paul did not assume that these believers were *"good to go"* since they had already underwent John's baptism (John, the forerunner). It was not about whether or not he assumed they were already "saved." It was about applying the next step; teaching them the deeper truths of the Gospel; allowing opportunity for them to become closer to God. And as the story affirms, Paul instructed these disciples to be RE-baptized in the NAME of Jesus! He knew that the name of Jesus Christ must still be applied. Let's observe the scenario:

> . . . Paul having passed through the upper coasts came
> to Ephesus: and finding certain disciples, . . . And he
> said unto them, Unto what then were ye baptized? And
> they said, Unto John's baptism. Then said Paul, John
> verily baptized with the baptism of repentance, saying
> unto the people, that they should believe on him which
> should come after him, that is, on Christ Jesus. When
> they heard this, they were baptized in the name of the
> Lord Jesus.
> —Acts 19:1, 3-5

Ask yourself: what was Paul's main concern?—*to find out the mode of baptism!* What did he instruct these people to do?—*to be RE-baptized in the name of the Lord Jesus!* Did Paul consider this matter to be of little concern since these people were already

Christians and had gone through a different baptism already?—*No, they still needed to be baptized again in the name of Jesus!* These are the principles in which the Apostle Paul taught; this is what he believed. This is a man who instructed the one-and-only body of Christ to . . .

> . . . keep the ordinances, as I delivered them to you.
> —I Corinthians 11:2

If we want to be of the same mind as the apostles then we must teach the same things to everybody; no matter if we have heard something contrary our whole lives; no matter if we believe we are already saved; no matter what denomination we may be affiliated with; no matter if those we preach to have been walking with the Lord for a hundred years or more. We must open our spiritual eyes and realize that, Satan, who is the god of this world (II Cor 4:4), does not want Christians to understand the significance of the apostle's baptism because he knows it is one of the absolute principles of Christianity (Heb 6:1-2). He knows it is an ordinance of God and that it is how we apply the name of Jesus Christ to ourselves. This is not a matter of determining "who's saved and who's not." It's a matter of understanding, humbly accepting, and willingly applying another principle that will draw us closer to God, no matter what position we may be in spiritually (just like Acts 19:1-6 teaches)! It's about taking the next step, bottom line!

Moreover, to answer the question, *"Why trust the apostles?"* . . . the answer is: *Because the entire Christian faith depends and is based upon the writings, beliefs, views, testimonies, teachings, and specific instructions (including baptism modes) of these men, who were witnesses of the Lord Jesus Christ. Our salvation depends upon the confirmations of these men!* And once again:

> How shall we escape, if we neglect so great salvation; which at the first began to be spoken by the Lord, <u>and was confirmed unto us by them that heard him</u>;
> —Hebrews 2:3

5

Turning Unto Fables

. . . That thou mightiest charge some that they teach no other doctrine, Neither give heed to fables and endless genealogies, <u>which minister questions</u>, rather than godly edifying which is in faith: so do.

—I Timothy 1:3-4

In studying the mystery of the Godhead I've only found that the more you contemplate the Trinitarian model—how God can be three "persons" but not three "gods"—the more it "ministers questions." I don't know if you believe in the trinity or not, but I do know that if you are reading this book then you probably have a hunger for God—or at least a curiosity of His identity. I also realize that you may be serving the Lord to the best of your ability and with the measure of knowledge and insight He has already given you. That's great! My desire nonetheless is to take you to the next level in your Spiritual walk—even to a higher calling—by revealing to you a clearer picture of what the apostles believed about the man, Jesus Christ. My hope is that you will achieve many "Spiritual Aha's" (as termed by some of my fellow brothers and sisters.)

Basically, I want things to start clickin' in your mind and stirring in your spirit. If you wish to take your God-given assignment above and beyond the norm—and if you want to do so by growing in knowledge and absolute Truth—then read on. On the other hand, if you do not want to be held accountable for anything deeper than what you already know—if you are content with your Spiritual walk and feel as though nothing further is required of you—then you probably shouldn't continue this journey. This covers some of the most eye-opening information about the Godhead that you may ever hear, and much of it may come as quite a shock. Overall, because we are talking about the true nature of God and understanding the identity of Jesus the man, we must all be in agreement that this is a matter of great concern.

Having said that, I'm just going to dive right into the topic of discussion by telling you what the apostles—the men who knew God as a man—did and did not believe. The apostles did NOT believe the Godhead consisted of three co-existent persons, who function co-equally and co-eternally. This is true because Trinitarian philosophies were not introduced to the world until *Scholastic Theology* began to surface *after* the ministry of the apostles. (Regarding theology: it's possible to have a four-year degree in knowing what the Bible *SAYS* and still not have the spiritual understanding to know what it *MEANS*.) While many claim, *"the trinity is biblical,"* most Bible scholars and historians would agree that the trinity doctrine didn't even exist among Christianity until nearly two centuries after the death of Christ; after the ministry of the original apostles had come to an end. While the following chapter reveals the historical aspect of how the triune-philosophy affected Christianity, this chapter presents two challenges which can be summed up in the following passage (and should be very familiar by now):

> <u>Study</u> to shew thyself approved unto God, a workman that needeth not to be ashamed, <u>rightly dividing</u> the word of truth.
>
> —II Timothy 2:15

➤ When *Studying* the Bible cover to cover it is very clear that a three-member godhead is NEVER mentioned, was never prophesied about, nor was it something Jesus or the apostles discussed or taught.

> When *Rightly Dividing* the Word of God it should become obvious that NONE of the apostles believed the man Jesus was a "separate person" or "co-equal member" who ruled *together* with or *alongside* God the Father.

To determine exactly what the apostles believed about the Godhead and Jesus the man one must disregard any philosophy which entered the church after the timeline of the New Testament writings (including the trinity doctrine). Only then will we be able to take Scripture for what it plainly teaches about the nature of God. In fact, to build a foundation we must first examine the Bible to determine exactly WHAT the Lord our God is. Notice:

> *God is a Spirit:* . . .
>
> —John 4:24

The Lord our God is a Spirit, an omnipresent being (Psalm 139:7-10), which means He is able to dwell anywhere He wants, whenever He feels like it, however He chooses to do so, and for whatever purposes He desires. Scripture proves that God has visibly appeared in one place, while being invisible in all other places. We can hear His audible voice from one corner of the earth while He is physically present in another corner of the earth (Matt 3:17). God does not have limits to what He can do or where He can appear, nor can He be contained into mere theories or philosophies dividing Him into separate persons. In the fewest and simplest terms Scripture teaches: God is a Spirit (John 4:24), and there is only ONE Spirit:

> There is one body, and one Spirit, . . .
>
> —Ephesians 4:4

The men who wrote the New Testament believed the Lord our God is ONE Lord (Mark 12:29) and that He is able to manifest Himself in as many ways as He chooses, whether physically visible or spiritually invisible (I Tim 3:16). The apostles believed the

Spirit of God is unlimited and that Jesus the man was a vessel to be used as a temple for the one and only Spirit of the Most High to dwell:

> For it pleased the Father that in him [Christ] should all the fullness dwell.
> —Colossians 1:19

As I previously mentioned, when viewing the New Testament writings we find that none of the early church members believed in the trinity. Frankly, because of historical *facts* which verify this teaching to not have yet existed during the apostles' ministry it would be unreasonable to believe otherwise. Nonetheless, because the Apostle Paul was aware of such philosophies potentially entering the church and causing confusion among the congregation, he chose to express his concern throughout his epistles. Notice his omen to the church (read this carefully as he invokes both a warning and a following affirmation):

> Beware lest any man spoil you <u>through philosophy</u> and vain deceit, <u>after the tradition of men</u>, after the rudiments of the world, and not after Christ. For <u>in him dwelleth all the fullness of the Godhead bodily</u>.
> —Colossians 2:8-9

In the passage above, Paul first warns the church of man-made philosophies and traditions. He then goes on by insisting that ALL the fullness of the Godhead dwells in the man Christ. He did not allude to the modern theory that *"Christ is only a PART OF the Godhead"* or a *"third member of the trinity."* He plainly insists that all of the fullness of God (who is a Spirit) dwelt within Christ the man. Unfortunately, even though Paul forewarned the churches of philosophies that would disagree with what he affirmed, Satan still understood something: Paul would not be around forever. In fact it wasn't until after the deaths of the early apostles that these new theories began to surface, thusly affecting the church by raising confusion and causing division. Men began to go beyond that which was written in order to bring new views into the church, though Paul specifically forbade it:

> . . . that ye might learn in us not to think of men above that which is written, . . .
>
> —I Corinthians 4:6

Paul understood the danger of considering the views of man in place of the Scriptures. That's why he differentiated such in the passage above. Nevertheless, as time went by and men continued to go beyond the Scriptures, modern theories began to surface the more church members questioned the logic of how God became a man. (Yet when *logic* is the determining factor in our view of the Godhead then we are more likely to question things in which our minds are *limited* to rather than allowing faith to dominantly influence us.) While the apostles understood that it was difficult to fathom how the Spirit of God became a man, they did not try to make it easier to comprehend by dividing the God into three persons. They simply understood the following:

> . . . great is the mystery of godliness: God was manifest in the flesh,
>
> —I Timothy 3:16

This is actually much simpler to understand than boggling your mind with the Trinitarian view, whereas it plainly states, *"God was manifest in the flesh."* God, who is a Spirit (John 4:24), became physically known unto the world through His fleshly incarnation, which He called "the Son" (Luke 1:3). The *Spirit* of God came to earth as the *Son* of God (I Tim 3:16). The *invisible* God became *visible* (Col 1:15).

Yet during the time shortly after the apostles' deaths the world began to see things differently. Instead of accepting the mystery in the passage above (how God Himself became a man) many began to accept what sounded more logical to the finite mind.

Therefore, the world began to hear many different philosophies of a three-member godhead, which, to some, made God seem more logical. Thus the trinity was born. And because it satisfied the human mind the *trinity* eventually became known as "the mystery"—taking the place of the true mystery. Even to this day if you were to ask a Trinitarian to explain how God can be three persons while still being one God he would likely say, *"It is a mystery; you can't understand it."*

But again, the Bible does not teach that the mystery is how God is three persons; nor did the apostles believe the mystery alluded to a three-member administration. If you notice two of the previous passages I've presented you should be able to detect exactly where the Bible clashes with the Trinitarian philosophy altogether. These passages alone should clarify the difference between what the trinity offers and what the apostles actually believed. While the trinity teaches that there are three *persons* who function together as one God, the passages above dictate the following:

- ➢ God, who is a Spirit, was manifest via human vessel (1 Tim 3:16). Simply put: God Himself became a man.
- ➢ Within a human temple, ALL the fullness of the Godhead dwelt (Col 2:10). Not just a third of God . . . *all* of who He is!

To better understand the minds of the apostle's one must first consider the various angelic forms and other theophanies in which God chose to present Himself throughout Scripture. Moses, for example, was able to hear the audible voice of God while he saw the visible manifestation we know as the *burning bush* (Ex 3:2-4). Additionally, many of us have read about God manifesting Himself through a pillar of fire and a pillar of a cloud (Ex 13:1). The first book of the Bible records God *walking* through the Garden of Eden (Genesis 3:8). Later in the book of Exodus we find that God spoke to Moses face-to-face just as a man speaks to his friend (Ex 33:11); though it is not specific as to assert the form in which He took on. And for considerable reasons it is commonly believed by many that Melchizedek, the Old Testament Priest, was actually a human theophany of God. Whatever the case may be, my point is this: we do not consider any of the Old Testament theophanies of God to be separate "persons" or "members" of the Godhead. Yet when it comes down to discussing the "Son of God," which is simply God's visible, human form (John 12:45; II Cor 4:4; Col 1:15; Heb 1:3) the majority refuses to take any other view than that Jesus the man is a literal, genealogical descendent of God the Father, thusly making Him a separate person (which forces him to be a separate god altogether).

I don't necessarily *like* to get caught up on minor technicalities, but I do believe it's relatively necessary when it involves knowing the Truth and discerning the difference between man-made theories. After all, we are talking about the true nature of God and understanding the identity of the man, Jesus Christ. We are dealing with a doctrine that either the apostles *did* or *did not* believe. Therefore, if we desire to understand God more completely then we must first realize that there is a difference between the two following concepts:

Concept #1—There are multiple manifestations of the one and only Spirit of God, which can be either visible or invisible; human or non-human (this is biblically sound).

Concept #2—There are three separate persons, having different personalities, sharing unity with each other, and they are all combined into one co-eternal, co-equal God, who function together and can be compared to an egg (this is a manmade idea).

Basically, the difference between the two doctrines is this:

➤ **Oneness-Christianity** (monotheism) teaches a distinction between body and Spirit within the Godhead yet does not classify these as "separate persons."

Trinitarianism (a form of tri-theism) teaches a distinction of actual "persons" or "members" among the Godhead yet justifies its tri-theism by using the contradictive statement, *"they are three-in-one."*

➤ **Oneness-Christianity** teaches that there are numerous aspects of God's nature and many manifestations or theophanies of His one-and-only *unlimited* Spirit.
Trinitarianism has taken three of God's manifestations and has categorized these as limited "persons" or "members" within their own boundaries.

Even though many Trinitarians will admit that the teaching of the trinity is not plainly offered throughout the Bible, the belief is *suggested* by what many believe to be indirect *implications, indications,* or *allusions* of three persons. Unfortunately we cannot afford to base our beliefs on what some people assume Scripture *implies.* We are not held accountable to subtle hints. The Word of God alone is our authority. What Jesus and the apostles plainly spoke or wrote about is what must be observed. Therefore, since the trinity doctrine is not in the Bible, nor did any of the apostles teach it, we cannot be condemned by refusing to believe in it. Actually, condemnation may come through quite the opposite: accepting something in which none of the New Testament figures offered. Quite frankly, because the trinity was introduced to the church nearly two centuries after Christ's ministry on earth, it should be obvious to everyone that it is an *addition* to Christian doctrine. And we should all know what the Word of God says about adding to it:

> What thing soever I command you, observe to do it:
> thou shalt not add thereto, nor diminish from it.
> —Deuteronomy 12:32

Not only does this verse clarify that additional teachings are unacceptable, it also states that we are to be careful to *observe* God's commands. Knowing this, let's observe the *first* of all commandments:

> And Jesus answered him, *The first of all the commandments is, Hear, O Israel; The Lord our God is one Lord:*
> —Mark 12:29

Now, this is probably our main clue as to what invalidates the triune-god philosophy altogether. Nevertheless, I must proceed to ask: if the first of all commandments states . . .

"The Lord our God is ONE Lord," . . .

. . . then why does the trinity teach, *"The Lord is three persons in one God"?*

Not only is the trinity an *addition* to the very first of all commandments, it is a *contradiction* to the command itself. Furthermore, because of Trinitarian tradition many churches have more or less made the first of all commandments ineffective:

> *. . . Full well ye reject the commandment of God, that ye may keep your own tradition. Making the word of God of none effect through your tradition, which ye have delivered:*
> —Mark 7:9, 13

> *Whosoever therefore shall break one of these least commandments, and shall teach men so, he shall be called the least in the kingdom of heaven:*
> —Matthew 5:19

How much more would you say that the first of all commandments applies to the passages above? This is quite a predicament. If we preach the Gospel using extra-biblical teachings then we must also know what makes these particular additions excusable, aside from all other additions. We need a valid justification to clarify why the Trinitarian model is acceptable while Scripture forbids it (Col 2:8-9). Furthermore, a Scriptural defense is needed to confirm by what authority we have made an exception for the trinity doctrine among our churches and why we have neglected the previous commands. In other words: if we are going to teach that God is a trinity of persons then it is only fair for the congregation to know its origin rather than leading them on to believe that *"the Bible portrays God as a three-in-one entity which cannot be fully understood"*—especially since people are more apt to accept whatever leaves "the preacher's" mouth instead of researching the Biblical nature of certain concepts themselves. Sadly, because too many people have neglected to research the trinity's origins it is most commonly assumed that, *"the Trinity supports Christianity, and it seems to be an accurate portrayal of God."*

We must keep an open mind and a heart of humility while learning about the trinity, because it may sting a little. I'm sure it has already come as a pretty big eye-opener for those who didn't realize the trinity is an *addition* to the Gospel and a doctrine that none of the apostles believed or taught. That alone can be pretty heavy to contemplate. On the other hand, we all may need to sit back and take a breather once we learn about its true foundation. History only confirms the trinity to be a teaching that entered the church during a time *when*—and around an area *where* (Acts 16:6-7)—tritheism (polytheism) and pagan mythology was highly influential. History substantially concludes that the trinity was an idea borrowed from paganism and combined with Christianity when the Roman government took over the faith. Even though Christianity was originally presented to the world by strict monotheistic apostles (confirmed by Scripture) the triune view of God unfortunately *seemed* to fit certain parts (not all) of Scripture. Consequently, many were deceived and followed this view. Considering the paganism involved with the trinity we must observe what the Bible says about combining paganism with our worship to the one and only true God and following their ways by imitating their worship:

> Take heed to thyself that thou be not snared by following
> them, . . . and that thou enquire not after their gods,
> saying, <u>How did these nations serve their gods?</u> . . .
> <u>Thou shalt not do so unto the Lord thy God</u>:
> —Deuteronomy 12:30-31

> Thou shalt not bow down to their gods, nor serve them,
> <u>nor do after their works</u>:
> —Exodus 23:24

Basically, we are forbidden to worship the gods of the world in ANY way, which includes imitating their evil practices. In essence Trinitarianism is an imitation of paganism and tritheism. It is a wretched attempt to serve the one and only God without letting go of worldly fantasies or mysticism. This strategy only brings God down to the level of secular religions and idolatry. And the Lord is very clear about His feelings:

> For thou shalt worship no other god: for the LORD,
> whose name is Jealous, is a jealous God:
> —Exodus 34:14

Let there be no mistake. I'm not implying that people are *intentionally* serving other gods by believing in the trinity. But we must realize that the *idea* of the trinity has blended secular religions with God Himself. It is the idea itself, the foundation that is so blasphemous to the Truth. When we entertain ideas that resemble the gods of other nations (Deut 12:30-31) this stirs up His jealousy.

> I am the LORD: that is my name: and my glory will I
> not give another, neither my praise to graven images.
> —Isaiah 42:8

Clearly God is not willing to share His glory with any other gods or persons, nor is He willing to share His glory even with *ideas* that are linked to other gods (II Cor 6:16). This applies to the manmade idea that divides Him into *"three persons who share unity"* (as many view it). On the contrary His command regarding pagan practice is:

> . . . but thou shalt utterly overthrow them, and quite break down their images.
> —Exodus 23:24

In essence and from a modern perspective we are to rid the church of this indignity. I understand that the vast majority of Christian churches probably view God as a trinity. I also understand that many are probably wondering how it can be a false doctrine when so many sincere Christians around the globe believe in this baffling phenomenon. Well, here is probably the biggest eye-opener yet:

> *And many false prophets shall arise, and shall deceive many . . . . For there shall arise false Christs, and false prophets, and shall shew great signs and wonders; <u>insomuch that, if it were possible, they shall deceive the very elect</u>.*
> —Matthew 24:11, 24

Undeniably, false teachers were foreseen to deceive Christians around the world; not only by those claiming to be Christ Himself but also those who have introduced false doctrines representing Christ. Moreover if the *"very elect"* were foreseen to be deceived then why should we assume otherwise? If we *truly* believe in what the Bible teaches then we shouldn't ignore or deny the reality that Satan works in our churches. We shouldn't be so naïve as to assume we *"couldn't possibly be subject to deception,"* especially when the Bible we claim to believe in so fervently warn us of these things. Quite frankly, if you personally cannot accept that Satan has permission to work in the churches—even to the point of deceiving the very elect—then I must inform you that he has succeeded and you have been deceived already. Ironically, the most typical mentality of someone who is deceived is, *"I'm not deceived."* Deception partners with denial; however, we mustn't deny the reality that Satan has been given permission to deceive the "very elect" by using man-made doctrines that *seem* right:

> There is a way that seemeth right unto a man, but the end thereof are the ways of death.
>
> —Proverbs 16:25

> And no marvel; for Satan himself is transformed into an angel of light.
>
> —II Corinthians 11:14

How much do we really believe in what the Bible teaches about Satan? How much do we believe that the previous passages could apply to us? How many of us are simply accepting the form of Christianity in which we have been presented with our whole lives, and how many of us are searching for Truth with all our heart? How many of us truly desire to understand the minds of the men who actually knew Jesus Christ?

Something very ironic that I mentioned earlier regarding those who hold fast to the Trinitarian philosophy is that they believe the Bible—though it does not *openly* or *directly* teach this doctrine—*indicates* or *alludes* to the notion that God is a trinity. Inconsiderably, many have concluded that the apostles actually believed in the trinity; they just *"didn't discuss it openly or directly mention it because it was common sense to them."* Yet if this were true then Scripture would not include the actual scenarios that disagree with this assumption.

We know there are only two possibilities: either the apostles were Trinitarians or they were monotheistic. Still, whichever view we assume the apostles believed the truth is that it had to be revealed to them somehow; they had to learn this truth for themselves. Therefore we must observe the scenarios in which Scripture offers. Notice, they learned how Christ is the *"express image"* of God (John 14:8-11), NOT a "member" of the Godhead.

Peter's revelation simply affirms that Jesus the man is *"the Christ, the Son of the living God"* (Matthew 16:16-17); NOT a *"co-equal, co-eternal individual functioning under God the Father"* (as some explain). And similar to Peter's words, the disciple Nathaniel simply stated,

> . . . Rabbi, thou art the Son of God;
>
> —John 1:49

This actually brings us to the most widely misconstrued perception of Jesus the man, whereas He is viewed as a literal, genealogical descendent of God the Father, thusly forcing His very being to exist as a totally separate person altogether. Hence we could not rightly say that He is God. Still, the Bible never teaches that the term "Son" refers to an actual descendent or literal son. Throughout Scripture the term "Son" is always used figuratively and simply refers to the *vessel* in which God chose to reveal Himself—the fleshly incarnation in which He used to be seen by man and to be used as a sacrificial instrument. In fact, Scripture teaches specifically *Who* the Christ is and *Wha*t the Son of God refers to:

> . . . Christ, who is the image of God, . . .
>
> —II Corinthians 4:4

> . . . his dear Son: . . . Who is the image of the invisible God, . . .
>
> —Colossians 1:13, 15

> . . . the express image of his person, . . .
>
> —Hebrews 1:3

In other words: the *Son* of God refers to the visible image of God's invisible Spirit; God's humanity. The apostles did not believe that God conceived a youngster in Heaven, who He then sent into the world in place of Himself. (That would only display a cowardice side of God; thusly we would have no reason to serve the Father since He would not have been the one who paid the ransom for our sins.) The apostles believed God Himself (who is a Spirit) came into the world *as* the Son (which was His flesh). They believed God's Spirit conceived flesh (Luke 1:31, 35), meaning Jesus the man cannot be a "co-eternal member" whereas His physical incarnation had a beginning (Luke 1:31, 35). Again, if Jesus the man is a separate person then He cannot be "co-eternal" with God the Father because there was a beginning to His physical incarnation, His birth. Physical manifestations come and go; but as for the unlimited Spirit of the One and only God:

> . . . I am the first, and I am the last; and beside me there is no God.
> —Isaiah 44:6

Compare the passage above to the following:

> *I am Alpha and Omega, the beginning and the end, the first and the last.*
> —Revelation 22:13

If God the Father and Christ were separate members in a tri-functional dictatorship rather than One unlimited divine being then—according to both passages above—apparently there is rivalry among the trinity. (According to trinitarianism the two statements above were spoken by two separate members of the trinity.) On the contrary, because Jesus Christ is God in the flesh and not a separate member (Is 9:6; 43:10)—because *Jehovah* of the Old Testament became *Jesus* of the New Testament—we can be fully rest assured that it is in fact the same One who stated this same claim but at different times.

Frankly, if Jesus the man is a separate *person* apart from the Father then we have absolutely no grounds for teaching that Jesus Christ is God; that, or else we would be forced to bluntly say that there are separate gods. We do not consider the titles *"Lamb of*

God" or *"Lion of Judah"* to be literal animals among the Godhead. We understand that these are figurative titles refering to the same God; therefore, why should we assume when viewing His title *"Son of God"* that *"God had a kid . . . Jehovah Junior."*? If we can understand the difference between *humanity* and *deity* (flesh and Spirit) then we should be able to understand the Oneness of God. In the simplest terms I can think of: *the human structure of God is the man Jesus Christ, while the Spiritual being of God dwelt within the man.* Notice:

> . . . <u>God was in Christ</u>, reconciling the world unto himself, . . .
>
> —II Corinthians 5:19

Contrary to Trinitarian philosophy none of the disciples viewed Jesus the man as a *person* or *member* of the Godhead, whereas not one scenario throughout Scripture mentions this. The trinity was not common sense to these men because the idea was a few centuries away from being introduced to the world. Even though many Trinitarians do not even know the origin of the triune-god theory many who have studied history (and do know) believe it was *"part of Scripture all along; it just went unnoticed until years later."* Basically, even though it was not taught in the early churches, discussed amongst any of the apostles in their epistles, or written about in any other New Testament manuscript whatsoever, many still believe the apostles *intended* to convey a portrayal of the trinity without straightforwardly teaching it. Conversely, this assumption is inconsistent with Scripture whereas Paul records:

> For we write none other things unto you, than what ye read or acknowledge;
>
> —II Corinthians 1:13

The passage above only affirms that there are absolutely NO implications, allusions, indications, or even suggestions; in other words, NO hidden messages throughout Scripture.

Theories suggesting the trinity doctrine to be Biblical are in direct contradiction to the passage above. Just as we discussed how alternate modes of baptism are extra-biblical, we see the same reality when observing the facts about the trinity doctrine: *Though the trinity doctrine may be taught from modern teachers by using portions of Scripture it was never actually taught by Jesus or the apostles during any single event in the Bible.*

The most tragic irony I can think of involving those who contend for the Trinitarian view is that many accuse Oneness believers of twisting the Scriptures to fit the Oneness doctrine. Yet—and because we've discussed the difference between biblical and extra-biblical teachings—this mentality is backwards whereas Oneness believers actually observe *first* what the apostles themselves taught while disregarding any philosophy they did not offer. In fact, disregarding man-made philosophies such as the trinity was a specific guideline in which the apostles instituted (Col 2:8-9). Conversely, Trinitarians disregard these guidelines throughout Scripture and rely upon philosophy in addition with *portions* of the Bible. In fact, the trinity is often explained by using sketches that were developed in attempts to understand it more accurately (since it so conveniently *"cannot be fully understood"*). Even so, here is a depiction of the most common diagram used to understand more clearly how three distinct persons can be one God:

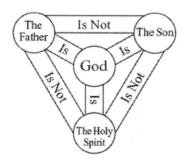

As if the trinity didn't already *sound* confusing enough by audibly hearing about it we are able to see just how contradictory it really is through the assistance of this visual aid. Not only does this affirm that the trinity doctrine teaches limitations and boundaries within God's characteristics and abilities, it more or less verifies that trinitarianism disregards the following guidelines:

> . . . we ought not to think that the Godhead is like gold, or silver, or stone, <u>graven by art and man's device</u>.
> —Acts 17:29

Likewise, and because the Bible speaks against views and representations devised by the skill of man, we should not picture the Godhead as being *an old white-haired man sitting on a throne accompanied by a younger dark-haired man on a second throne next to him with a bird flying around*. Notice:

> Thou shalt not make unto thee <u>any graven image</u>, or any likeness of <u>any thing that is in heaven above</u>, . . .
> —Exodus 20:4

Clearly we are not to conjure up our own ideas (graven images) of what God is like; let alone teach others to do so. In view of the illustration above, the trinity teaches that the Father is God, but the Father is *not* the Son. And this applies to each so-called "person" of God. Each *"person"* is God, but each person is not *each other*. Still, a major flaw with this theory is that the Bible clearly refers to the *Son* and the *Father* as being the same One:

> For unto us a child is born, unto us <u>a son is given</u>: and the government shall be upon his shoulder: and his name shall be called Wonderful, Counsellor, The mighty God, <u>The everlasting Father</u>, The Prince of Peace.
> —Isaiah 9:6

Notice that the Holy Ghost (Counselor) is also mentioned in the same verse. This is a very problematic issue among the Trinitarian faith. Sadly, many will continue to ignore these contradictions. If the three "persons" are each God but not each other, wouldn't that mean God is not God? Can God actually not be Himself? This is nothing more than a delusional paradox. Either there are three separate gods or there is only one God. There cannot be both. We cannot mix the world's philosophies with the church. We cannot blend tri-theism with monotheism. Notice:

> Ye cannot drink the cup of the Lord, and the cup of devils: ye cannot be partakers of the Lord's table, and of the table of devils.
>
> —I Corinthians 10:21

So which one is it? Is God really not God? Is each "person" partly God? Or is God really just one in Himself? (The response you are likely to receive from a Trinitarian is *"Don't question it; you can't fully understand the trinity, it's a mystery."*) But why in the world would God have us to believe there are *"three separate persons of God, but not three separate gods"*? No wonder people claim the trinity *"cannot be fully understood."* How is it that people would rather accept a contradictive man-made philosophy rather than to just believe what the Bible openly states (Deut 6:4, Mark 12:29)? Moreover, the diagram clearly and inarguably portrays that God is *divided* into three separate persons. Now, if you didn't already know, God cannot be divided:

> . . . Every kingdom divided against itself is brought to desolation;
>
> —Luke 11:17

If God Himself is divided into three limited persons within their own boundaries then shouldn't everyone start searching for another god whose kingdom won't crumble? Think about it: as humans made in God's image we are able to distinguish our own flesh from our mind and our spirit, yet we do not consider ourselves to be three persons in one. Make sense? Likewise, why should we stoop to believe that there are three *persons* in the Godhead rather than just accepting that there are numerous *aspects* of His nature and multiple manifestations of His one and only Spirit? The only way we can truly know the identity of God today is by taking His Word for what is *plainly* written in it; teaching what the apostles taught without considering the views, ideas, contradictive charts and other illustrations of mankind, which entered the world after the lives of the apostles. The fact is that there is only One Lord and one belief system (Eph 4:5), which was first spoken by the Lord and confirmed unto us by the apostles (Heb 2:3). And the Bible says there is *no excuse* for believing anything contrary, even about the Godhead:

> For the invisible things of him from the creation of the world are clearly seen, being understood by the things that are made, <u>even his eternal power and Godhead; so that they are without excuse</u>:
>
> —Romans 1:20

To Whom Did Jesus Pray?

We previously examined that the apostles believed it was a *mystery* how God was able to be both *Spirit* and *man* at the same time (I Tim 3:16). They did not question the logic of Jesus' prayers or think that it must take multiple members in the Godhead for this to be possible. Considering *everything* written by the apostles they simply understood that when God appeared here on earth in the flesh, He, as our example, was a visible, audible, and spiritual representation, who showed them how to pray. They even asked Him, *"Lord, teach us to pray"* (Luke 11:1). When God Himself entered the world as the Christ, He identified with us through His own experience as a human. When Jesus Christ prayed it was His flesh responding to His Spirit. When Jesus became human He understood first-hand the difference between our fleshly nature and the will of the Spirit (Gal 1:3-4). Jesus not only set the example as He prayed, He also identified with us when He prayed:

> Forasmuch then as the children are partakers of flesh and blood, he also himself likewise took part of the same;
>
> —Hebrews 2:14

Since God became like us in order to set an example we should therefore observe His example and apply it to ourselves. Through this we should see how we are to interact with the Spirit of God. Conversely most Trinitarians gather something totally different. Rather, those who believe in separate persons of God believe Jesus' prayers illustrate one person's *relationship* with the other. Trinitarians typically assume Christ's prayers were to teach us about the "Father-Son" relational status among these two members of the trinity. However, this brings up one of the most observable inconsistencies in the Trinitarian faith. Trinitarians believe that God the Father is the father of the member called *"God the Son"* and a separate person from the Holy Ghost altogether. Therefore, we must look to the Scriptures to confirm exactly *who* the father of Jesus Christ truly is (keep in mind, Trinitarians believe the Father and Holy Ghost are two separate persons). The problem, however, is that when Trinitarians teach that the Father is the member who conceived Christ they have not considered that the Bible actually teaches it was the Holy Ghost who conceived the child:

> . . . she was found with child of the Holy Ghost . . . . for that which is conceived in her is of the Holy Ghost.
>
> —Matthew 1:18, 20

Now, if Jesus' prayers were to exemplify a father-son relationship among the Godhead—and since Trinitarians do not believe the Holy Ghost is the same person as the Father—then according to this belief Jesus Christ did not know which member of the trinity was His father. However from the apostles' perspective—taking the New Testament writings for what is *plainly* written in them—we are able to observe that Jesus Christ's physical conception was not a matter of one "person" begetting another, neither were His prayers from one "member" to the other. Conversely, and from a different perspective, by understanding that *Spirit begat flesh* we are also able to understand that *humanity prayed to deity*. Christ's interaction with the Spirit of God should not be mistaken as *"one person's relationship to another person"* whereas His prayers were to exemplify how we ourselves should respond to God; how our physical being connects with the spiritual realm.

Basically, this is what is NOT taught in Scripture but is what Trinitarians believe:

➢ One member of the trinity prayed to the other (two "persons" interacting)
➢ It is a mystery how God is three cooperative persons but not three gods

Now, this is what IS taught in Scripture and is what the apostles believed:

➢ Jesus the man prayed to God (Jn 17, etc) who is a Spirit (Jn 4:24)
➢ It is a mystery how God is both flesh and Spirit (I Tim 3:16)

If we claim to believe in the trinity—clinging to the belief that there is a distinction of persons or members in Heaven—then, because there is only one God (Deut 6:4), we are forced to choose from one of the following options:

➢ Jesus the man is not God (and His claims were false)
➢ There are actually multiple gods (and the Bible authors, who were strictly monotheistic, were mistaken)

The Comma Johanneum

> For there are three that bear record in heaven, the Father, the Word, and the Holy Ghost: and these three are one.
>
> —I John 5:7

While the passage above may seem to support the triune-god philosophy by stating *"there are three"*, the truth is that there is no *three-in-one* formula in Scripture that was actually written by the apostles. In truth, the passage above is not included in any of the early Greek manuscripts of the New Testament. (Seriously, look it up.) This verse was not actually written by the Apostle John. History books attest that this passage originated from an early Latin scribe, who simply jotted this passage down as a marginal notation. As time went by his memo became customary in the Latin Vulgate. During the sixteenth century a Greek scribe by the name of *Desiderius Erasmus of Roderdam* was persuaded by the Catholic Church to include this passage in his *Textus Receptus Third Edition* (Greek New Testament, published in 1522), even though there were no preexisting Greek manuscripts containing the passage.

Some English Bibles include this passage, and some do not. For that reason many Trinitarians who know the origin of this passage will not use this verse as a defense to support his or her beliefs, whereas it is unsubstantial. On the other hand Trinitarians who do *not* know the origin of this passage will not hesitate to use this for support of his or her beliefs. (This is why we are instructed to know the origin of our beliefs (II Tim 3:14).)

In view of what we covered in the previous chapter it seems rather peculiar when considering that the two most prominent verses used to support the Trinitarian philosophy (Matt 28:19 & I John 5:7) are known to be victims of Scriptural interpolation by the Catholic Church. Nevertheless, even though this was the devils attempt to alter sound doctrine we are still able to see right through this scheme. Look again to the passage above and consider what this could apply to while taking into account the monotheistic view of the apostles. Once again we must realize that when the apostles spoke of God they did not distinguish the Father and the Son as separate persons; only operative demonstrations of His one and only Spirit. Again, they believed God is a Spirit (John 4:24) with different titles given to express His various manifestations and purposes. For instance:

➢ FATHER: His intimacy and relational status to us; our Provider to whom we call upon in prayer.
➢ SON: His plan of deliverance and salvation; our visual, audible, and spiritual example of how we are to conduct ourselves on earth.
➢ HOLY GHOST: His operational and instructional activity; our Teacher. His promises and gifts are set in motion by His Spirit.

One God (Deut 6:4), one name (John 17:26, Acts 4:10-12); but somehow the word *"persons"* seems to always make its way into every triune explanation of I John 5:7. Still, even if this passage actually *was* a part of the original manuscripts (given that John did write this), essentially it supports the Oneness of God more substantially by acknowledging that the three most recognized *aspects* of God's nature are one. Consider the following:

➢ God is a Spirit (John 4:24)
➢ There is only one (selfsame) Spirit (I Cor 12:11, Eph 4:4)
➢ When Scripture refers to the Holy Spirit (or Holy Ghost) this refers to the same Spirit of God *manifesting* Himself unto mankind, not a distinct person.

> I will pray the Father, and he shall give you another Comforter, that he may abide with you forever; . . . I will not leave you comfortless: <u>I will come to you</u> . . . . and <u>I will . . . manifest myself to him</u>.
> —John 14:16, 18, 21

While Trinitarian philosophy teaches that the Comforter is another "person" the fact is that He is simply referring to another manifestation or role of the same, unlimited Spirit of God. The Holy Ghost is no more of a separate "person" of God than the pillar of fire He used to reveal Himself to Israel. And Jesus the man is no more of a separate person of God than the burning bush. Again, it's all about different manifestations of the one and only Spirit of God. If you can understand the difference between flesh and Spirit then you can understand the mystery of the Godhead. When Jesus spoke of His Father He was not referring to another member. He was simply speaking of His invisible Spirit, which dwelt within His body, the one and only "person" of God (Heb 1:3).

> *Believest thou not that I am in the Father, and the Father in me? the words that I speak unto you I speak not of myself: but the Father that dwelleth in me, he doeth the works. Believe me that I am in the Father, and the Father in me:*
> —John 14:10-11

The identity of Jesus Christ becomes clearer when one can understand that God's Spirit became flesh (I Tim 3:16) rather than assuming that *"one 'person' literally sent another person to the world."* Truth becomes more explicit when a person realizes that *all of the fullness* of the Godhead is in Jesus Christ (Col 2:9) rather than believing He is only a *"third, co-equal deity."* And it becomes more life-changing when you can appreciate that Jesus Christ is the *express image* of God (Heb 1:3) rather than a "member" of a three-part God.

The Writer's Testimonies

> And when I saw him, I fell at his feet as dead. And he laid his right hand upon me, saying unto me, *Fear not; I am the first and the last: I am he that liveth, and was dead; and, behold I am alive for evermore,*
> —Revelation 1:17-18

The Apostle John actually saw a vision of the express image of God just as He is now and how we will see Him in the end. The Book of Revelation entails specific details about John's vision of the Lord, yet none of these writings include more than ONE person or member of the Godhead. John specifically states that he saw *ONE* throne and only *ONE* who sat on the throne (Rev 4:2). He did not believe in another or literal throne at the *"right hand of God"* whereas this phrase had not yet been twisted in a literal sense. As a matter of fact Bible scholars and historians would agree that the phrase "right hand of God" has always been a part of many dialects of foreign languages, including Greek, Hebrew, and Aramaic and that it has always referred to nothing other than a position of authority and power but was never meant to be taken literally. And in this case God's authority and power was manifested through His physical incarnation, the man Jesus Christ (Matt 28:18), who is the image of the Spirit of God:

> Who being the brightness of his glory, and the express image of his person, . . . when he had by himself purged our sins, sat down on the right hand of the Majesty on high;
>
> —Hebrews 1:3

In fact I remember hearing a fellow minister of the faith who shared his thoughts on the phrase *"right hand of God."* His statement:

"If one suggests that this phrase is to be taken literally then he has not considered the obvious fact that God is an omnipresent Spirit (John 4:24, Psalm 139:7-10). Every time Scripture refers to the physical attributes of God (aside from His human incarnation) it is metaphoric or emblematic. Because God is a Spirit, He therefore does not have literal or physical body parts, including a right hand."

The John 1:1 debate . . .

> In the beginning was the Word, and the Word was with God, and the Word was God.
>
> —John 1:1

While many would misinterpret this passage by teaching that "the Word" refers to a distinct and totally separate person who was with God, we must understand that this is not what is written. If this were the case then we could not rightly say that this "person" is God, as John 1:1 goes on to say. Otherwise there would be more than one God. In essence, think about two people standing next to each other. While they may be "with" one another, the reality is that they both cannot be the same person.

In reality one must first determine what the *"Word"* is before concluding anything further. Originally, the word *"Word"* derived from the Greek word *"Logos,"* which means: *thought, expression,* or *plan*. Now, we know that God had a predetermined plan of salvation for mankind (Acts 2:23). It was this premeditated *plan of redemption* that was "with" God in the beginning; His plan to become human, to take away the sins of the world. And at the appropriate time His plan came into effect, it was put into action:

> And the Word was made flesh, and dwelt among us, . . .
>
> —John 1:14

We must not think that there was a separate person with God in the beginning. The Amplified Bible even states: *"the Word was God Himself"*. God Himself was made flesh and dwelt among us. To think the *"Word"* refers to another person is only an opinion based upon assumption and human philosophy. None of the author's of the Bible intended to convey this notion, whereas we see that God's Word contradicts this through the writings of Moses:

> See now that I, even I, am he, and <u>there is no god with me</u>:
>
> —Deuteronomy 32:39

The Bible affirms that the Bible authors were absolutely assured of the existence of only one person of God:

> Unto thee it was shewed, that thou mightiest know that the LORD he is God; <u>there is none else beside him</u>.
> —Deuteronomy 4:35

Think about this: Moses spoke "face-to-face" with God (Ex 33:11). Before his death he completed the first five books of the Bible, including the account of creation, the flood, the life of Abraham, etc. If God was a trinity of persons then Moses either failed to recognize this or he failed to write about it. The only instance where he reveals anything linking numerical standing with God is when he wrote, *"The Lord our God is ONE Lord"* (Deut 6:4).

Additionally the prophet Isaiah was a man who heard from God. He is known to have the most considerable foresight of the promised Messiah. His writings affirm the following. Thus saith the LORD:

- ➤ I am the first and the last; and beside me there is no God (Is 44:6).
- ➤ My glory will I not give to another (Is 42:8).
- ➤ I am the Holy One of Israel; thy Savior (Is 43:3).
- ➤ My servant whom I have chosen; that ye may know and believe me, and understand that I am He: before me there was no God formed, neither shall there be after me (Is 43:10).

Also King David assures us that he had never heard of a three-in-one God:

> . . . for there is none like thee, neither is there any God beside thee, <u>according to all that we have heard with our ears</u>.
> —II Samuel 7:22

> . . . thou art God <u>alone</u>.
> —Psalm 86:10

If God was a trinity of persons then this is something in which every author of the Bible was unaware of. As for the men of the New Testament, we have only two options:

➤ They failed to fully grasp the true character of Jesus the man as being a literal, genealogical descendent of the Almighty Father.
➤ Or else they *did* grasp the triune nature of God but failed to clarify this to the world.

New Testament author, Luke, claimed to have a *"perfect understanding of all things from the very first"* (Luke 1:3). Not once did he mention in his writings (the Book of Luke and The Acts of the Apostles) that God is a tri-operative family of entities. His understanding—taken from his Gospel, Luke 1:35—was that:

➤ Spirit birthed flesh.
➤ This manifestation of the Spirit would be *called* "the Son of God."
➤ The very *reason* Jesus was called the Son of God is because of how he entered the world (via human birth).

In further support of Luke's testimony we cannot ignore the fact that the name *"Emmanuel"* holds the meaning *"God with us"* (Matt 1:23). God literally formed a physical representation of *Himself,* thusly calling this vessel the "Son of God." Christ is the visible *image* of the invisible God (II Cor 4:4, Col 1:15), not a member of a three-part godhead.

New Testament writer, James more or less suggested a "Duh" attitude in his epistle. He writes how even the devils understand the oneness of God (Js 2:19). Overall, if the physical manifestation of God's Spirit was a separate person then we would have no cause to serve any of the other "persons" because the other two so-called "members" did not sacrifice themselves for our sins. Ultimately, because there is only one person in the Godhead we are able to be fully rest assured that the God we serve is not only the One who created us; He is also the One that became a human and sacrificed *Himself* for our sins. God Himself became like us:

> Forasmuch then as the children are partakers of flesh and blood, <u>he also himself</u> likewise took part of the same; . . .
>
> —Hebrews 2:14

Men and brethren, if God is a trinity of persons then we are forced also to believe that there was a flaw in the original Gospel; that is, until the post-apostolic apologists of the second, third, and fourth century *improved* it with their new and updated philosophies—ideas in which the original apostles apparently overlooked.

The Spiraling Perplexity

A good friend of mine and sister in the faith, America Nevitt once wrote:

"Many people would look at this view [Oneness] *and say that it is "carnal" and that we cannot even begin to understand something as complex as the Trinity . . . . But why would God make such a fantastic mystery out of Himself and who He really is if the Bible is here for the purpose of us being able to know Him to His fullest capacity? To know Him the best that we can, why would He seek to hide that from us? The answer is that He doesn't. We as humans have been confused by the teachings of many who allowed themselves to be deceived by their own carnal minds . . ."*

Well said! Even though the Bible teaches that the "mystery" is how God became flesh (I Tim 3:16), as a result of human philosophy it was finally decreed by Rome in the year 325 AD that the *mystery* was now how God could be three persons *AND* one God at the same time. Government decided for itself that the only logical explanation of God is:

God is a three-member trinity, yet this phenomenon cannot be fully understood.

Isn't that quite convenient? Any question which may arise could be answered by simply stating *"We cannot fully comprehend this mystery."* Even to this day those who agree with the Trinitarian philosophy are convinced that the three-in-one explanation of God is absolutely *"phenomenal . . . yet baffling."* The majority has been persuaded that the *"triune-god"* explanation is accurate, yet they also believe that the *"three-in-one"* formula *itself* is too baffling to comprehend. Notice the suspicious nature of this mentality as it is quite deceptive. Many are convinced that the trinity *explains* God, but at the same time they believe the explanation itself is too complicated to fathom. Clever yet deceiving! It is believed to be the answer, yet the answer cannot be understood. That's deception at its prime! People no longer believe the phenomenon is how God Himself became a man (like I Timothy 3:16 says); they now believe the phenomenon is how God is simultaneously *"three persons AND one person."* Seriously, how can deception *not* be a factor when people are so easily convinced that God can be three persons under the justification that, *"It just cannot be understood by the human mind"*?

As I mentioned in chapter two, we shouldn't think the mysteries of the Gospel were intended to *remain* a mysteries (Mark 4:11). Even though a mystery is something the finite mind cannot *fully* understand it is also something in which can only be revealed by the Spirit of Truth. And while we are expected to devote our lives to accumulating these bits and pieces of Truth to form a clearer picture of the mystery, *we have no cause to search when we are convinced that we already have the answer*. Make sense? When we believe that we already have the mystery figured out then we have no reason to seek the identity of God any further. That's the danger! That's the deception! The trinity doctrine has convinced people to settle for less. When we accept the trinity doctrine as Truth then we have set the boundary as to where our insight will end. Satan uses this doctrine to convince people that the Godhead is *"too confusing to understand."* Yet God's desire is that we come to know Truth (I Tim 2:4) through the revelation of Jesus Christ:

> And <u>this is life eternal</u>, *that they might know thee the only true God, and Jesus Christ, whom thou hast sent.*
> —John 17:3

Furthermore, Jesus assures us that *unto us it is given to know the mysteries of the Kingdom of God* (Mark 4:11). Again, the areas that Satan is most likely to confuse the world about are not only the areas that relate to *salvation* but also the areas which directly affect our understanding of *who God is.* And according to the passage above knowing the identity of God and understanding His manifestation as Jesus the man plays a major role in gaining eternal life. Therefore we must obtain clarity of absolute doctrines of the Bible in order to discern the difference between man-made philosophies. Yes, both doctrines (Oneness & Trinitarianism) claim that it is a "mystery" when it comes to the more inexplicable concepts. And it is true that both doctrines must be taken by faith. Yet there is a difference between having faith that God's Spirit became flesh (as I Tim 3:16 teaches) and having faith in a contradictive manmade philosophy which cannot decide whether God is three or one (the trinity).

I will say it again: we must understand that deception itself is more deceiving than we've come to realize because of how rare it is that a person recognizes when he has been deceived. Prime example: Someone once claimed that *"Even though the trinity doctrine is not biblical we still need it to understand who God is."* (Apparently he had never ventured into II Timothy 3:16-17, which teaches that we can be made complete by the Bible itself (or Colossians 3:8, which warns us of human philosophies in the first place).

I am reminded of a quote in which I recall hearing from a good friend and minister of the faith, Brother Travis Jones. His statement: *"I often wonder how the world can be so naive as to believe in only one devil . . . but three gods."* Remarkable! Men and brethren, God is complex, but He is not complicated. And there is no human philosophy that will allow us to understand the nature of God more than God's Word itself. Just because God's Spirit dwelt among His flesh does not mean it involved another "person." Even the devils all know it doesn't take three persons for God to be God:

> Thou believest that there is one God; thou doest well: the devils also believe, and tremble.
>
> —James 2:19

Keep the passage above in mind as it directly relates to the following point of discussion. As this chapter separates the traditional, modernized view of God from what the apostles actually believed, we now come to what separates *true* Christianity from Trinitarianism (which is a secular form of Christianity).

Christianity: based upon what is *clearly* and *plainly* written in the Bible (II Cor 1:13); not by what people assume Scripture indicates or alludes to. The Bible is the canonized, historical, textual accounts of the apostles, including the words and actions of Jesus Christ and His elect who were given authority to carry on His Message, by word of mouth and by letter (II Thess 2:15) and shows which doctrines they themselves taught. They all believed, preached, and even commended others for believing "God is ONE."

Trinitarianism: a secular religion of pagan mythology and Wiccan culture that was added to the Gospel of Jesus Christ during the second century. It was formulated by a man named *Tertullian* (surf the web; look up the name) roughly over a century after the New Testament writings were completed. Trinitarianism was later sanctioned by the Roman government in the year 325 AD as the only legal form of Christianity, a.k.a. Roman Catholicism.

❖ The Network:

> Now the Spirit speaketh expressly, <u>that in the latter times some shall depart</u> from the faith, giving heed to seducing spirits, and <u>doctrines of devils</u>;
>
> —I Timothy 4:1

Even though the majority of churches today view God as being three persons, the apostles did not believe this. They did not believe in combining philosophical suggestion with Christianity (Col 2:8). They believed *Christianity was Christianity* and *tri-theism was tri-theism*. They believed *one is one* and *three is three*. They didn't believe in both:

> Ye cannot drink the cup of the Lord, and the cup of devils: ye cannot be partakers of the Lord's table, and of the table of devils.
>
> —I Corinthians 10:21

Consider the following:

➢ Christianity was founded upon Jesus Christ (I Corinthians 3:11); trinitarianism was founded upon sheer philosophy.

➢ Christianity was confirmed by the apostles (Hebrews 2:3); trinitarianism was later presented to the church by a non-apostle.

➢ Jesus and the apostles were monotheistic (Mark 12:29, James 2:19); Tertullian was tri-theistic.

➢ Jesus cannot change (Malachi 3:6, Hebrews 13:8); however, Tertullian attempted to change Him.

➢ Christianity is based off what is written in the Bible (II Tim 3:16); trinitarianism was added to what was *already* written in the Bible.

The circumstances of those who have a hard time giving up the idea of the trinity are quite ironic. Many of us feel that if we acknowledge the trinity doctrine to be false then we would be admitting that we understand *less* about God. On the contrary, by recognizing and admitting the trinity to be a philosophical fable actually proves that we understand *more* about the nature of God than when we were duped in the first place. Again, it's not a matter of understanding the distinction of "persons"; it's about understanding the difference between the *flesh* and the *Spirit* of the one and only God. I would much rather know the Truth and be left with a few questions than to accept a fable and deny that I'm totally puzzled! Make sense?

The bottom line is that the Bible never says *"God is three persons in one God!"* I will say it again: God is complex, but He is not complicated! It's quite ironic that mainstream Christianity can accept that Jesus predicted *many* false representations of Christ to arise and deceive the very elect (Matt 24:5, 11, 24); and how the Bible speaks of men twisting the meaning of Scripture (II Peter 3:1); and how the words of Christ state *"wide is the gate and broad is the way that leadeth to destruction"* (Matt 7:13); yet when faced with the facts, these same people cannot accept that the *many* "Christian" denominations we see today have fulfilled His very words by yoking themselves with this distorted view of who God is. Again, there is only . . .

> One Lord, one faith, one baptism, One God and Father
> of all, who is above all, and through all, and in you all.
> —Ephesians 4:5-6

When represented by Trinitarianism, Christianity is reduced to nothing more than *another secular religious system*. I encourage each of you to visit the library or surf the internet to uncover (in more depth) the trinity's origins. Understand what took place prior to these philosophies which minister more questions than they are worth. Don't be fooled any longer by this delusion of the enemy. Don't just *"accept it."* Try to feel the heartbeat of the Apostle Paul as he constantly warned his dear friends and the saints of the churches about this:

Beware lest any man spoil you through philosophy and vain deceit, <u>after the tradition of men</u>, after the rudiments of the world, and not after Christ. For <u>in him dwelleth all the fullness of the Godhead bodily</u>.

—Colossians 2:8-9

The Triquetra

. . . we ought not to think that the Godhead is like gold, or silver, or stone, graven by art and man's device.

—Acts 17:29

The triquetra is a symbol that originated from various pagan religions. Additionally it is shared by Wiccan culture (witchcraft & psychics). Not only is it affiliated with satanic practice; it is also the representational symbol for many mystical goddesses. It was adopted by the Roman Catholic Church during Medieval Times and was used to represent the trinity.

Today we see that, not only is this symbol used in Celtic body art (tattoos), it is also on the covers of many Bibles. What an extreme variation of beliefs tied into this wile of the enemy (including the Christian faith)? Nonetheless, I highly doubt that the One-and-Only God is pleased to see many churches sharing a symbol that is used to represent a vast amount of secular religions. Remember, the Lord will not share His glory with any other (Is 42:8). I challenge each and every reader to research the origin of this symbol for his or her self to see the dark reality behind it all.

6

The Powers That Tickled Our Ears

... and the government shall be upon his shoulder:
—Isaiah 9:6

Government has always been a burden to Christianity, but its effect was undoubtedly the most radical around 325 A.D. when Catholicism was brought into the scene. Despite the fact that nothing could ever stop the Gospel Network from continuing steadfastly, Satan did his best using the trinity doctrine and alternate baptism methods—because they conveniently complemented one another—to alter the Gospel of Jesus Christ. Intended to be deadly poisons, these alterations acted more as numbing agents to the Christian faith.

Still there is an answer as to *how* and *why* these doctrines became so accepted in the church—why these distortions became the most recognized icons of the Christian faith. And while the obvious answer is *'Satan'* as he knew this is what the world would eventually consider to be "normal" when viewing Christianity, he still needed someone with power to help him; someone who had the ability to make everything seem rational and the power to prove everything to be beneficial. Before we discuss the figure I'm referring to please allow me to briefly reflect on a few men who God considered to be *His* chosen vessels.

➢ Simon Peter: The lowly fisherman. Because of his social status he was basically considered to be insignificant. The average person would not have thought listening to him would have been worth his or her time no matter what his message was. Therefore he shouldn't have had any influence on the world whatsoever (logically speaking). Still, Jesus gave him the keys to the Kingdom of Heaven and chose him to launch the church (Matt 16:17-18).

➢ Matthew: A disciple, who wrote the first book we see in the New Testament. Although, prior to his ministry he was a tax collector, which automatically would have placed him under the status of a social outcast and a lowlife hated by many (possibly hated even by some of the other disciples at first). It is highly unlikely that any of his peers thought he would actually leave his old ways behind to later write a Gospel which would be universally read.

➢ The Apostle Paul: A man whose former acquaintances (Pharisees) were the same people that rejected their own Messiah. Why would anyone who knew Paul personally have wanted to accept what he had to say about Jesus Christ (Acts 23)? Furthermore, before his ministry and once Christianity began to spread across the region he was devoted to eradicating the Christian faith altogether. Yet he allowed God to transform his heart and mind, which thusly resulted in his planting of many regional churches for God.

God is able to use the most unlikely people imaginable to spread His Gospel, while Satan typically uses people with an extensive amount of influence. Because Satan does not have the power himself (nor does anyone) to destroy the body of Christ, he does the best he can with influential figures. For those who study end times, keep this in mind while studying on the subject of the antichrist and the false prophet (Rev 16:13; 19:20). They too will be loved by the world. But for now, please allow me to introduce a powerful political figure, who seriously impacted not only the world but also those of the Christian faith:

Constantine "The Great"

(Flavius Valerius Constantinus)
A.D. 274-337

> Now I beseech you, brethren, mark them which cause
> divisions and offences contrary to the doctrine which
> ye have learned; and avoid them. For they that are such
> serve not our Lord Jesus Christ, but their own belly;
> and by good words and fair speeches deceive the hearts
> of the simple.
>
> —Romans 16:17

Just to give you a brief overview of this guy, he was the first claimed Christian emperor of Rome, who basically compiled paganism, politics, and Christianity to form Catholicism. Let there be no mistake, his main focus was not to spread the Gospel; his overall goal was to build an empire bigger and better than any other. Nonetheless, because Christianity was the most renowned controversies in the world during this time, Constantine saw a perfect opportunity to use this to develop his own religious form of government. Again, as we cover the highlights we must understand that Constantine's goal was NOT to improve Christianity; it was to improve his own interests.

Formerly raised to believe in the Roman gods familiar to his era, Constantine eventually converted to Christianity; though many still question the true nature of his faith. He proclaimed to Rome his faith in Christ, though he didn't actually take the steps toward salvation until he learned he was going to die. Throughout the course of his life, he often related (or rather confused) false pagan gods with the one true God, Jesus Christ. He claimed to have not only seen visions of the Roman sun god known as Sol, he also claimed to receive dreams from Jesus Christ. (When considering that not only God Himself, but also mythological figures were supposedly communicating to this man in dreams, this alone should raise questions.) His most legendary dream recorded was of Jesus appearing to him, prophesying that he would be the victor of a battle against his opponent Maxentius. Coincidentally he did in fact defeat his rival, which is what influenced his decision to convert to Christianity.

It is already known to many that during this time severe forms of persecution succeeded, whereas many Christians were being killed left and right. We see many examples even in the Bible how the name of Jesus Christ led to the death of Christians (Steven for example). Those, who hold firmly to the *name* of Jesus Christ, will always be the number one targets for persecution (II Tim 3:12). But even though Constantine fought against persecution and eventually legalized Christianity, his own personal interests seemed to be the spark in his motive. Ironically, the organization he was constructing would later become the most prominent persecutor of true Christianity in history. While many consider this man to be "Great" because he legalized Christianity, what is typically ignored is that he irreverently modified the Gospel during the process. His method was basically a conditional agreement in that Christians were forced to compromise the foundation of the original doctrines in order to be accepted. As you will see Constantine obviously did not base his decisions according to what is written in the Bible. His show of godliness was just a way to become wealthy. In essence . . .

> Perverse disputing of men of corrupt minds, and destitute of the truth, <u>supposing that gain is godliness</u>:
> —I Timothy 6:5

Constantine's allegiance to the church was a conspiracy (Eph 6:12), whereas he had ulterior motives. His intent was not so much to restructure the *church* by means of using the government; on the contrary, his objective was to improve *government* by using the church. He did this by taking advantage of people who didn't know any better; people who—like Constantine himself—wanted to serve their own personal interests. He basically offered his own version of stimulus-packages to the public. Those who submitted to his regulations—anyone who wanted to profit—must first and foremost be a member of the church that he was gaining control of. These incentives would have benefited any man who held a position in office, especially since an office position in itself may have been a perk for some. In essence, the Roman Catholic Church was formed to some extent through bribery; that, and capitalism. Nevertheless . . .

> THEREFORE seeing we have this ministry, . . . we faint not; But have renounced the hidden things of dishonesty, not walking in craftiness, not handling the word of God deceitfully; but by manifestation of the truth . . . But if our gospel be hid, it is hid to them that are lost: In whom the god of this world hath blinded the minds of them which believe not, . . .
> —II Corinthians 4:1-4

If I could just go ahead and remove the veil; Constantine's method was actually Satan's scheme to welcome the world into the church (or to pollute Christianity). This was a strategy designed to further corrupt everything and is another example of one of his many cunning methods. Maybe some of these career-driven officials could have been able to see what was going on had their priorities been set on ecclesiastical affairs rather than imperial. These men were primarily focused on whatever would assist them in climbing to the top of the corporate ladder. Nonetheless, the routine of showing up to church for an hour a week wasn't really that big of a deal.

Basically—if I could break it down even further—they were going to church for the wrong reasons, not to get close to God. If you have ever studied the history of the Catholic Church, you have more than likely come across the event known as "the Council of Nicaea," where bishops came together, and basically tried to figure out the best way to build this church; how to operate it through the state (by governmental standards rather than Biblical). While there are many indications of certain Catholic traditions (other than triune baptisms) even before Constantine's time, that doesn't mean Catholic rituals are Biblical. On the contrary, pagan rituals were adopted and combined with other man-made religions to form Catholicism. Constantine just happened to be the man who paved the road, which resulted in the first government-structured house of worship (vain worship): The Universal Roman Catholic Church.

❖ The Network:

> And I saw, and behold a white horse: and he that sat on him had a bow; and a crown was given to him: and <u>he went forth conquering, and to conquer.</u>
> —Revelation 6:2

Now, before we discuss this council meeting allow me to first point something out about the passage above; something very noteworthy. There are only two white horses mentioned in the book of Revelation; one in the previous passage, depicting Catholicism, and one in the following passage depicting our Lord Jesus Christ:

> And I saw heaven opened, and behold a white horse; and he that sat upon him was called Faithful and True, and in righteousness he doth judge and make war.
> —Revelation 19:11

This is a perfect example of how our struggle is not against flesh and blood, but against the powers of this dark world and the spiritual forces of evil (Eph 6:12). Notice the similarity? Satan, who is known to disguise himself as an angel of light (II Cor 11:14), would do anything to confuse the world about true Christianity. Though true doctrine was given to the apostles nearly two-thousand years ago—including the truth about salvation and the identity of the Godhead—Catholicism claims to be the one true church of God even though she modified, altered, distorted, and admonished most essential apostolic truths nearly three centuries after the true foundation was laid. And while the "Abomination of Desolation" is commonly known to many as the event of the Antichrist claiming to be God on the temple mount; we see another illustration of this act, which has continually been occurring for nearly seventeen-hundred years already. The Catholic Church, who *claims* to be the church in which Jesus died for, has fulfilled the following words of Christ:

> *Then if any man shall say unto you, Lo, here is Christ, or there; believe it not. For there shall arise false Christs, and false prophets, and shall shew great signs and wonders; insomuch that, if it were possible, they shall deceive the very elect.*
> —Matthew 24:23-24

Before we discuss the Nicene Council let's consider first something very interesting. The Book of Acts actually reveals that there was much spiritual warfare going on among this geographical region (Acts 16:6-7). It only makes sense that Nicaea (Bithynia) was—if you didn't already know—known as the *Factory of Religions* during this era. When taking that into consideration it becomes even more eye-opening to see how the spiritual forces of evil have contaminated true doctrine. We have already covered the doctrines of alternate baptisms and the trinity doctrine, but what must be observed is how these new theologies influenced the minds of the council. During this meeting (Nicaea) the overall goal was to assemble the first traditional, man-made rule-based church, by using governmental order for the structural backbone. Yet they still needed to figure out how to combine tradition with Truth, which cannot be done without committing blasphemy (Mark 7:7-9, 13).

Nevertheless, because the trinity was the propaganda of the century they simply used it as a foundation. Yet at the same time it continued to raise questions among the public (as it still does to this day). Ever since Tertullian brought the idea that three separate persons make up one God everyone was confused. The council tried to figure out whether or not the Holy Spirit—being a separate "member"—was equal to the Father and if the Son was co-eternal with the others. Keep in mind that rather than looking to the Word of God for direction, the council based this whole conversation on a theory of a trinity. Even so, they discussed the possibilities:

"Is the Holy Spirit a separate being altogether . . . I mean, apart from the Father?"

"Is it maybe, kinda, sort of the same substance as the Father?"

"And just exactly what makes Jesus the man co-eternal with the other two people in the godhead? Isn't His physical beginning recorded in Scripture?"

"Isn't His body, mind, and Spirit just the same as 'this-that-and-the-other'?"

"Well, if that's the case then maybe they are all 'one' something or another, but who really knows?"

"Whatever! Let's just decide on something so we can present it to the public, alright?"

"Okay, we'll go with Tertullian's philosophy and call it a 'three-in-one' god since it appears to fit the Bible better than some of the other theories we've heard?"

"Sounds good; let's just alter a few Scriptures first and then tell everyone it's a 'mystery' which nobody can fully understand. That way this will compensate for the Scriptures we overlook ourselves or can't explain!"

"that actually sounds pretty convincing already."

"Love It!"

"Ok, great; let's do it!"

"All in favor, say 'I'." . . .

"I!" . . . "I!" . . . "*I!*" . . . "I!" . . . "I!" . . . "*I!*" . . . "*I!*"

Though the example above may be a sarcastic paraphrase of the actual conversation, the topic of discussion is *no* exaggeration. Notice the similarity in the following passage.

❖ The Network:

> . . . but [they] became vain in their imaginations, and their foolish heart was darkened. Professing themselves to be wise, they became fools, And <u>changed the glory of the uncorruptible God into an image</u> made like to corruptible man, and birds, and fourfooted beasts, and creeping things.
>
> —Romans 1:21

Basically, once the trinity was introduced to the world the Roman government used it as an icon to represent their new Christian-based, man-made religion. They just needed to figure out a logical explanation before they could promote it. But even *that* wouldn't be too difficult as long as they could convince people it is a "mystery" in which the human mind cannot fathom.

Think about this: we've seen various *conspiracy theories* involving our modern day government, many of which have been written into books, making very successful sellers. These often-popular narratives are attractive to the public whether they are true or false. The worst part is that these cover stories often pertain to incidents in the world that cannot be changed, and sometimes don't even matter. Although that doesn't change the fact that we love to get to the bottom of the stories by whatever means necessary. And even though the motives of those who cover these stories are often driven by the desire to add drama to the scene the overall goal is to find the source of truth.

My point: maybe we should have the same attitude toward the *salvation plan* and the *trinity doctrine*—meaning that we should have the desire to detect the truth by getting to the core of the problem; *knowing the origins of our traditions.* Our motive, however, should be to stand for Truth glorifying God for who He is and what is written in His Word; what the apostles actually preached. Even though the trinity doctrine and alternate salvation plans are part of most denominational churches today, that doesn't change the fact that they are the biggest sugar-coated governmental cover-ups in history and do *not* agree with what the apostles first presented.

I urge everyone to research the origins of his or her own doctrinal belief to uncover the Truth. If you cannot trace everything back to the Bible then something is wrong. And as we are presently doing so we have learned thusly that during this era (the Dark-Ages) a contaminated form of Christianity is what became tolerable. At this point in time a person would have been considered to be an outlaw if he were to preach Truth according to the apostles' doctrine. If a person wanted to be accepted then he would have to play by the rules of Constantine, which was nothing more than a toned-down, diluted form of lukewarm Christianity. Actually, we should not think that Catholicism is even a remote form of Christianity considering that we were warned of its destruction to the one true church of God.

❖ The Network:

> For <u>a nation is come up upon my land</u>, strong, and without number, whose teeth are the teeth of a lion, and he hath the cheek teeth of a great lion. <u>He hath laid my vine waste</u>, and <u>barked my fig tree</u>: he hath made it clean bare, and cast it away; the branches thereof are made white.
>
> —Joel 1:6-7

To understand the prophecy above more clearly we must first remember what Jesus taught the apostles. His words:

> *I am the vine, ye are the branches, He that abideth in me, and I in him, the same bringeth forth much fruit: . . . If a man abide not in me, he is cast forth as a branch, and is withered; . . . but I have chosen you, and ordained you, that ye should go and bring forth fruit, and that your fruit should remain: . . . If they have persecuted me, they will also persecute you; if they have kept my saying, they will keep yours also.*
> —John 15:5-6, 16, 20

Even though the Roman Catholic Church wasted the vine and ruined God's fig tree by stripping away the fruits of the Spirit and adding doctrines of devils to the Gospel, there is nothing that could ever strip away the Word of God, which is forever. Let's take a look at the following passage, which are the comforting words of Jesus.

> *And I say unto you my friends, Be not afraid of them that kill the body, and after that have no more that they can do.*
> —Luke 12:4

During the time when Roman Catholicism advanced more prevailingly throughout the land those who were willing to bear the name of Jesus—in agreement with the apostles' true teaching—could expect to be tortured and burned alive. As a matter of fact the Catholic Church has killed more Christians—numbering at 68,000,000 murders—than any other persecutor, due to the fact that these saints contended for the truth and would not submit to her politics.

❖ The Network:

And upon her forehead was a name written, MYSTERY BABYLON THE GREAT, THE MOTHER OF

HARLOTS AND ABOMINATIONS OF THE
EARTH. And <u>I saw the woman drunken with the</u>
<u>blood of the saints, and with the blood of the martyrs</u>
<u>of Jesus</u>:

—Revelation 17:5-6

I know many of you may be thinking this suggestion is a
little far-fetched; however, when reading through the book of
Revelation chapters 17 & 18 it becomes evident—through
knowledge of historical figures and events—that Catholicism
is unmistakably "the Mother of Harlots." While many people
conclude various theories of who she may be we must understand
that she is a spiritual force. Some believe famous monuments fit
the profile (Statue of Liberty), and some hold to the notion of
actual persons. Nonetheless, our struggle is not against flesh and
blood; it is against rulers of the dark world and against spiritual
wickedness in *high places* (Eph 6:12).

Something very eye-opening to consider is what the Apostle
John foresaw and recorded in his epistles. First he writes that the
early saints were *expecting* antichrists, which were actually at work
already (I John 2:18). Also he states that antichrists will arise from
within the church (I John 2:19). He then identifies antichrist as
being a *spiritual* force (I John 4:3) in which there are *many* forms
(I John 4:4). The overall purpose of this dark force, he writes, is to
deceive (II John 7). Not only will this force deny the Truth about
the Godhead (I John 2:22; 4:3) but it will strive to lead the saints
away from Truth (I John 2:26). Nevertheless, if we abide in the
true doctrine of Jesus Christ we shall overcome (II John 9).

As we previously discussed Revelation 6:2 depicts the Catholic
Church, whereas she impudently defies God by placing herself in a
position of recognition (the white horse); a position in which only
the Lord Jesus Christ deserves. (By the eighth century people had
even begun kissing the Pope's feet.) I am reminded of a minister
and teacher of the apostolic faith, who pointed out the following
verifications linking the Catholic Church to the "woman."

> ➤ The pope wears white (the horse) and adorns himself in gold
> ➤ He sits on a throne made of gold
> ➤ Cardinals are attired in red and adorn themselves in gold
> ➤ Bishops and archbishops are attired in purple and are adorned in gold
> ➤ Catholic Church members wear pearls around their necks (rosaries)
> ➤ Catholic sanctuaries and cathedrals are decked in ornaments of gold and other precious stones (candlesticks, communion instruments, furniture)

❖ The Network:

> And the woman was arrayed in purple and scarlet colour, and decked with gold and precious stones and pearls, having a golden cup in her hand full of abominations and filthiness of her fornication.
>
> —Revelation 17:4

The passage above depicts a vast similarity when considering the previous points. And when viewing the Catholic Church and its demeanor it becomes even more evident that she positions herself above all others:

> How much she hath glorified herself, and lived deliciously, . . .
>
> —Revelation 18:7

Unfortunately, the majority will continue to deny the reality—even the possibility—that something so abominable could be happening before their very eyes. But again, this is where we must ask ourselves how much we really believe in the Word of God; how relevant it is to the people, places, and events throughout the world; how *alive* Scripture truly is (Heb 4:12). Basically, the question is: *"Do we honestly have as much faith in the Bible as we claim"*? If we can believe what the Bible says about the devil being a deceiver and the father of lies then why is it that we so easily overlook what he has been doing in the churches over the past seventeen hundred years? The answer is because Satan, who disguises himself as an angel of light, would have us believe that any form of Christianity is acceptable in the sight of God, even though the original church forbade such.

Notice Revelation 17:4 states that the woman held *"a cup in her hand full of abominations and filthiness of her fornications."* Just for a moment let's think about what the Lord's Supper or "communion" represents. It symbolizes the salvation plan in which Jesus established through His death, burial, and resurrection; salvation in which we also receive by following Christ through our repentance, baptism in His name, and by receiving the Holy Ghost. In essence, the Catholic Church offers her cup of abominations by teaching an alternative plan of salvation. Furthermore, she has prostituted herself with various pagan beliefs (including tri-theism), which in turn represents her fornication. Because of these distortions to the Gospel Christianity was becoming everything opposed to what it was founded upon.

By 500 AD the world had entered the Middle Ages, or commonly known as the "Dark Ages," which is very appropriate considering that mainstream Christianity was as far from the Truth as the Bible predicted. The world became spiritually naïve, the Pope gained control over Europe, and the right to read the Bible was forbidden. The government outlawed personal ownership of the Holy Scriptures in order to make any textual revisions needed to further support Catholicism.

Nevertheless . . .

Truth Sprouts

Not only does the Bible prophesy about the destruction of the early Apostolic Church it also forecasts its *Reformation* and full *Restoration*. And what has taken place in the past 2,000 years has indisputably coincided with what the Bible predicted. We need to understand that the signs of the *End of the Age* are presently occurring, and part of prophecy is the *Restoration* of the true church of God.

❖ The Network:

> And <u>I will restore to you</u> the years that the locust hath eaten, the cankerworm, and the caterpiller, and the palmerworm, my great army which I sent among you. And ye shall eat in plenty, and be satisfied, and praise the name of the LORD your God, that hath dealt wondrously with you: and my people shall never be ashamed.
>
> —Joel 2:25-26

One way of breaking down (not twisting) this prophecy would be to say that—because it refers to the Restoration of Truth—it describes how false doctrine (trinity, baptism in titles) would be widely exposed in the last days. More specifically how the saints of the latter times would receive revelation—through immense studying (II Tim 2:15) and historical archive digging (Rom 15:4)—as to what doctrines were originally present in the New Testament church and which doctrines are extra-biblical. The problem in the Dark Ages was that too many people were so Biblically naïve, and were unable to see what was happening in the world around them . . . until one day . . .

> . . . *The seed is the word of God.*
>
> —Luke 8:11

As I previously mentioned the right to own a copy of the Holy Scriptures was out of the question during the Dark Ages. However, during the 1400's the printing press was invented, which in turn played a major role in Bible distribution. As the world began to have more access to the writings of the apostles many began to notice significant flaws in the Catholic system. The passage above signifies one man's observance of what is written in the Word of God. Martin Luther was a man who observed the ludicrous *Catholic* principle that we can *"buy our way into Heaven."* Many are already familiar with this I'm sure, so for those who don't know any better: the Catholic Church sold pardons to the public. Basically, a person could buy remission for his sins! Obviously this was nothing more than a fundraiser; however, Martin Luther just happened to notice this discrepancy and contended for that which he knew was right. Not that he wanted to start a rebellion or anything; Luther just wanted to get together with some fellow believers to discuss some of these systematic flaws, which eventually resulted in Protestantism.

From that point forward, the world began to see many different forms of denominations throughout the course of time: Catholic, Orthodox, Lutheran, Anglican (Episcopalian), Presbyterian, Methodist, Nazarene, Baptist, Adventist, cultic divisions, a few in between, and finally, the Nondenominational church, which is just an attempt to beat the system. (Obviously the Nondenominationalist's realize that the Bible speaks against division; however, instead of having a standardized structure, these organizations devised a solution that basically invites *any* form or denominational belief. Basically, it's a *"believe whatever you want as long as you attend here"* type of mentality. It's basically a form of denominationalism which is unofficial and goes unannounced. But this is a totally different subject).

Moreover, we see that over the course of time the *Reformation* of the church was fulfilled in phases. And once the Pentecostal experience became widespread throughout the world once again it led to the final phase of the *Reformation*, which was the *Restoration* of the *apostles'* church. Restoration did not have its fulfillment through new teachings or false revelation. While many assume that the modern apostolic movement was *formed* through new man-made doctrines, the fact is that it *resurfaced by removing man-made teachings* which contaminated the true doctrine to begin with. It was fulfilled because over the course of time people began to see different truths in Scripture, which steered them back to understanding the original teachings of the apostles. Obviously the issue of *Jesus-name-baptism* is one of the final revelations of this fulfillment. And because this teaching remained hidden for so long—even though it is undeniably true—many people today have a hard time accepting it to be the *only* mode of baptism bound in Heaven. Additionally it is the same with the trinity doctrine. Because this is the most prominent icon of modern Christianity many have a hard time accepting the apostles' monotheistic view of the Godhead. Yet what is vital in our understanding is that when Scripture speaks of committing fornication with the Mother of Harlots (Rev 18:3) it refers to those who have accepted man-made doctrines and traditions in exchange for apostolic Truth.

The Reformation has been a continual process of many phases throughout the past 500 years with many denominations. Ultimately, these denominations would only play roles in the gradual process of reforming the original church of God, which is a fully-restored church that preaches the Truth about salvation (which some churches *are* closer to the Truth than others). Restoration comes through both knowledge of the past and revelation of Truth by understanding what the Scriptures foretold. The apostles knew that men would bring in new theologies and philosophies that would seem right unto man; however, Proverbs 16:25 teaches that man has always done what he thought was right in his own mind, while the consequences of his actions only lead to death.

Church Restoration comes through understanding where exactly in history the church drifted away and knowing which philosophies caused the most confusion in the church. Many people look around at all the different churches and wonder which one is right. Actually, we shouldn't view it as *multiple-choice;* we should think more along the lines of *True-or-false.* What many people don't realize is that the Bible tells us which church is the one true church of God. According to the Bible the true church of God is identified by whether it preaches Truth; it is recognized by whether it preaches the *Salvation Plan* according to what was established by the church of Acts: *Repentance, Baptism in Jesus' Name, and the Infilling of the Holy Ghost.* In the words of my pastor:

"The book of Acts is a set of blueprints as to what the church today should be."

Very true; and according to the Bible the Apostolic Church we see in the book of Acts is the same church that was prophesied about being restored in the last days:

> And I will restore to you the years that the locust hath eaten . . .
>
> —Joel 2:25

The outpouring of the Holy Ghost is part of it:

> And it shall come to pass afterward, that I will pour out my spirit upon all flesh; . . . And also upon the servants and upon the handmaids in those days will I pour out my spirit.
>
> —Joel 2:28-29

Peter quoted this same prophecy, just before he proclaimed the plan of salvation to the world (Acts 2:16-17). And there shouldn't be any differences between the church found in the book of Acts and the church of today. Wouldn't you say the churches most likely to be approved by God are probably the ones that resemble the church in the Bible the most; the churches that are *contending for the faith that was first delivered to the apostles* (Jude 3)? When considering the apostolic movement of today we can adequately conclude that the Restoration of the one true Church of God is clearly being fulfilled before our very eyes whereas the world is presently receiving the latter rain of the Spirit:

> . . . Behold, the husbandman waiteth for the precious fruit of the earth, and hath long patience for it, until he receive the early <u>and latter rain</u>.
>
> —James 5:7

The events that have taken place over the past century; the immeasurable outpourings of the Holy Spirit; countless Pentecostal revivals; and the plethora of churches planted in the world whose saints stand firm in the apostolic doctrine (Acts 2:42) and standard plan of salvation (Acts 2:38); these accurately describe the Remnant of people, who God said would be a part of the latter rain. These happenings are definite signs of prophecy fulfillment and confirm what the prophet Joel documented: *"And I will restore to you the years that the locust hath eaten."* And just to set the record straight (and this is the most important part), the term *Apostolic* does not refer to a denomination; it is an adjective used to describe the doctrine of the apostles. If you are not familiar with the term *Apostolic* then allow me to briefly enlighten you on its meaning and usage. Webster's Collegiate Dictionary, 11th Edition defines the term APOSTOLIC: a) *of or relating to an apostle*; b) *of, relating to, or conforming to the teachings of the New Testament apostles*. This term is used by various authors, Bible scholars, theologians, and historians to describe either the *doctrine* of the apostles or the *time frame* or *era* of the early church.

The New Testament church was obviously an apostolic church, given that it was started by the apostles. The Apostolic Church—whether or not one refers to the early Apostolic Church or today's Apostolic Church—simply refers to the church of the apostles. Again, the word "apostolic" simply means "like the apostles" or "apostle-like." One shouldn't be alarmed to hear this term, whereas it is Biblical. Some versions of the Bible use the term *Apostolic*, some use the term *Apostleship*, and some simply use the word *Apostle*. Today, the apostolic faith is basically a continuation of the apostles' church and is based upon EVERYTHING in which they wrote in the New Testament, not just bits and pieces or portions of Scripture. While many denominationalists believe certain models throughout the epistles only applied to the early church, the Apostolic Church today applies anything the Bible offers. The Apostolic-Pentecostal movement of today is not a part of the denominational mainstream, whereas it is a continuance of the New Testament church. (And they did not divide themselves into sects.) Allow me to further break it down.

The early Apostolic New Testament Church did NOT consider itself to be:

➢ Trinitarian (*a combination of monotheism and tritheism*)
➢ Catholic (*universal*)
➢ Denominational (*divisional, sectional, more than one*)
➢ Orthodox (*conformist, conventional, traditional, mainstream*)
➢ Nondenominational (*informal denominationalism*)
➢ Universalist (*find your own path, believe whatever you want*)
➢ The Church of Jesus Christ of Latter Day Saints (*Mormons*)
➢ The Watchtower Organization (*Jehovah's Witnesses*)
➢ "Religious" (*lacking relationship*)

God has always had a crowd, but He still knows who the church is and who his saints are (John 6:64-71). The types of churches listed above are not mentioned in the New Testament writings, nor were they around during the early apostolic era; though it's God's desire even for these to come unto the knowledge of Truth (I Tim 2:3-4). These types of churches resulted from uniting Catholic philosophies and traditions with Christianity. These types of churches—though some are closer to the Truth than others—offer a worldly perspective of the Gospel.

> For they are not all Israel, which are of Israel:
> —Romans 9:6

The Apostolic-Pentecostal Church of the New Testament DID consider itself to be:

➢ Oneness; monotheistic (Is 9:6, Matt 1:23, Mk 12:29, Col 2:9, I Tim 3:16, Js 2:19, Rev 22:13)
➢ Pentecostal (Acts 2:1-4; 8:12-18; 10:44-48; 19:1-6, etc)
➢ A church with the truth about salvation (Matt 16:17-18, John 6:68, Acts 2:38)

➤ A separated church who practices holiness (II Cor 6:17, Rom 12:1-2, I Peter 1:15-16, I Thess 5:22, I John 2:6; 5:21, Heb 12:14, etc)

➤ A church who has not forsaken the name of Jesus Christ by removing it from the one and only baptism (Eph 4:5, Acts 2:38; 8:12,16; 10:48; 19:5; 22:16) bound in Heaven (Matt 16:18-19)

➤ The one and only church of the living God; the pillar and foundation of Truth (I Tim 3:15); the only church in which God established

The Apostolic-Pentecostal Movement of Today is:

➤ A continuation of what happened throughout the book of Acts and the rest of the New Testament (II Tim 3:14)

➤ It is a fulfillment of prophecy; the last phase of church restoration; back to its original state (Joel 2:25-26)

➤ A church that preaches the primary steps toward salvation just as the apostles of the New Testament: repentance, baptism in Jesus' name, and the infilling of the Holy Ghost (Acts 2:38)

➤ A church who believes the Lord our God is ONE Lord (Deut 6:4)

How Dare They?

Before we continue any further I would like to briefly point out that the historical accounts we've covered—when tied in with Scripture—undeniably validate the suggestions I've presented in this book. Yet I also believe that when considering the attitudes and opinions of spectators toward those of today's Apostolic-Pentecostal movement many tend to have bitter feelings toward this particular church body. From what I've noticed it's more socially acceptable to be affiliated with the denominational mainstream and *"agree to disagree"* than it is to actually follow in the footsteps of the apostles by *contending for the faith*. Society tends to have more tolerance and acceptance towards organizations that are further away from the Truth. Allow me to break it down even more by offering just a few examples (please do not mistake this as *"bashing other churches"*):

> - Denominational Churches (these are only a few examples)
>   - Baptists—everyone loves Baptists!
>   - Methodists—warm feelings, generally
>   - Nazarenes—nobody seems to mind
>   - Lutheran, Wesleyan, Presbyterian, etc—to each his own
> - Non-denominational Churches: A modern, casual, and alternative form of Christianity widely accepted by the vast majority
> - Cultic-Christian Churches and other communities
>   - Mormons—nobody really cares
>   - Jehovah's Witnesses—usually ignored
> - The Universalist Church: A step further away from the non-denominational church, whereas you can believe *whatever* you want, and it is the truth; yet nobody seems to speak against this outrage
> - The Catholic Church—the Mother of Harlots: though she is the very reason the early church underwent a period of destruction in the first place, her irreverent practice seems to have become the most respected form of Christianity when viewed by the world

Now, I understand that every individual may have his or her own opinion about the organizations I've presented above. However—though it may seem stereotypical—these are the attitudes in which I have personally observed. The overall point is that these various divisions are usually viewed as, *"Just worshiping God the way they feel comfortable doing so. To-each-his-own."* But when considering the attitudes of others when Truth is being affirmed, people tend to become angry when being told they

NEED to be baptized in order to be saved; especially when being told it must be *"In Jesus' Name."* If you try to tell someone they NEED to receive the Holy Ghost in order to be saved it seems to be an outrage, even though this was the apostles' initial approach (Acts 19:1-6). And here is the connection:

> But these speak evil of those things which they know not:
> —Jude 10

Even though the early New Testament church underwent severe persecution for preaching the same things—Repentance, Baptism in Jesus' Name, the infilling of the Holy Ghost, and the Oneness of God—people seem to overlook the cosmic similarity of the Apostolic-Pentecostal movement of today, who not only preaches the same Message and practices the commands of God the same way but also suffers the same ill-treatment. Now ask yourself: Am I hated for what I believe? Honestly, are you? Jesus openly stated that we would be hated for being his followers (Matt 10:22, Mark 13:13, Luke 21:17). But how many of you are actually hated for what you believe in? I dare say that if you are not hated for what you believe then you are not doing enough for God, and you may not even be a part of the body of Christ at all. It seems like the more Catholic traditions a church practices, the less it is hated. Notice, the following two illustrations are just a few themes in which the Bible constantly offers throughout its many chronicles written:

➢ If you are a part of a promise, you're going to be persecuted
➢ History always repeats itself

Considering the above themes I dare say that NO church today, other than the Apostolic Church, is able to truly identify with the following allegory in which the Apostle Paul applied to the early church.

❖ The Network:

> Now we, brethren, as Isaac was, are the children of promise. But as then he that was born after the flesh persecuted him that was born after the Spirit, even so it is now.
>
> —Galatians 4:28-29

As for the Catholic Church: not only has she contaminated true Christian doctrines, she also has raised her children to believe the same lies and to practice her abominations. Consequently, those who partake in her iniquities shall receive of her plagues:

> For all nations have drunk of the wine of the wrath of her fornication, and the kings of the earth have committed fornication with her, and the merchants of the earth are waxed rich through the abundance of her delicacies . . . . Come out of her, my people, that ye be not partakers of her sins, and that ye receive not of her plagues. For her sins have reached unto heaven, and God hath remembered her iniquities.
>
> —Revelation 18:3-5

Look back to the passage above. First of all it teaches that ALL nations are guilty of committing fornication with her. Her doctrines have become widespread over the past seventeen-hundred years and have affected the various church establishments throughout the globe. Nevertheless, because everything the Bible prophesies about comes to pass, there is a fully-restored body of believers whose mission is to reveal that which the Mother of Harlots has veiled from the saints. Therefore, no matter what our current circumstance may be, we must *"come out of her."* In other words, we are to let go of every doctrine she has used to contaminate the true doctrines of Jesus Christ; we must reject any form of participation with her. We must DE-denominationalize, DE-nondenominationalize, DE-Catholicize and disaffiliate ourselves from any cultic-Christian organization. No doubt, we must *"come out of her."*

I recall a certain occasion when the Catholic Church of a local community sent out invitations to the surrounding denominational churches. The purpose was to assemble together and lay aside our differences in order to have an ecumenical service. (They even stated openly that they did not wish to convert anybody.) Those who were blind to Scriptural prophecy—including a number of pastors—accepted the invitation and participated. The service consisted of singing and prayer but nothing pertaining to absolute doctrine from the Word of God (because nobody was in agreement).

As I stated in the introduction, conviction is more or less the reason why Christianity has caused more controversy in the world than any secular religion; it only occurs when Truth is affirmed. This is probably why these churches chose to lay aside their differences and ignore the very reason we are supposed to gather together in the first place! Nonetheless, coming together and ignoring the problem of division only places our stamp of approval on having doctrinal differences all the more! This whole attitude which basically says *"Let's gather together so we can convince ourselves that there is no division among Christianity"* only confuses people even more about what is true and false. Imagine what it would have been like if the scattered nations of old gathered back together in attempts to complete the Tower of Babel. Many groups of people, who don't even speak the same language, trying to accomplish a common goal—it's hopeless! Make sense? Furthermore, the Bible speaks against blending doctrines. Observe John's forewarning:

> If there come any unto you, and bring not this doctrine, receive him not into your house, neither bid him God speed: For he that biddeth him God speed is partaker of his evil deeds.
>
> —II John 10-11

By welcoming doctrines of Catholicism into our churches we are partaking of evil. Catholicism changed not only the identity of God (the trinity) but she also altered the covenant of salvation using triune baptisms. She introduced doctrines and traditions such as infant-baptism and sprinkling (416 AD), worship of Mary (451 AD), kissing the Pope's feet (709 AD), worship of physical symbolic objects, artifacts or relics (786 AD), Canonization; declaring the dead as saints (995 AD), prayer beads—imitating paganism (1090 AD), The commencement of the Great Inquisition (1184 AD), purchasing forgiveness of sins (1190 AD), the doctrine of Purgatory (1439 AD), Mary's Immaculate Conception doctrine (1854 AD), priestly mediator-ship declared as the ONLY way to receive forgiveness of sins (1985 AD), etc. The list goes on! Inevitably, because she transgressed and failed to abide in the original doctrine of Christ she therefore does not have God (II John 9). The most tragic irony is that those who partake in her fornications—those who are yoked with her false doctrines—speak evil of those who are trying to help them understand Truth. Nevertheless, this reality was foreseen in advance. Observe the Network once again:

> For the time will come when they will not endure sound doctrine; but after their own lusts shall they heap to themselves teachers, having itching ears; And they shall turn away their ears from the truth, and shall be turned unto fables.
>
> —II Timothy 4:3-4

7

What Itching Ears Must Conclude

That in the dispensation of the fullness of times he might gather together in one all things in Christ, both which are in heaven, and which are on earth; even in him:
—Ephesians 1:10

I understand it may come as quite a shock to some that what this book offers is contrary to everything you may have ever known about true Christianity. A common dispute among mainstream Christianity is: *"How can you say that only one church is the right church?"* The answer is because the apostles believed this (Eph 4:4-6). They did not believe in divisional sects or denominations (I Cor 1:10) who preach different doctrines of salvation. If we are to say that every church under the Christian name is a part of the same body then we have automatically disregarded the Biblical concept of UNITY altogether. If we avoid the principle of *unity* by placing our stamp of approval on various churches who preach diverse doctrines then we are hypocrites.

As a matter of fact if you *do* consent to having a variety of churches in the world who preach alternative routes to God then you do *not* totally agree with the apostles and more than likely you are *not* part of the same body as they. When you don't share the same views, teach the same doctrine, or practice the same customs as these men (who wrote the Bible) then you are probably a part of a totally separate establishment altogether, even though you may go under the "Christian" name. Nonetheless, Jesus foretold that many would come in His name and would deceive even the very elect (Matt 24:5, 11, 24). Notice the following passage, and consider to whom this may apply:

> . . . wide is the gate, and broad is the way, that leadeth to destruction, and many there be which go in thereat:
> —Matthew 7:13

Referring to the passage above many do not believe that Jesus was identifying Christian churches but that He was referring to worldly sinners who do not know or follow Him. Yet Jesus affirms just a few verses later that He *is* speaking of those who claim to be "Christians" whereas they claim to have done many works in His name. Notice:

> Not every one that saith unto me, Lord, Lord, shall enter into the kingdom of heaven; . . . Many will say to me in that day, Lord, Lord, have we not prophesied in thy name? and in thy name have cast out devils? and in thy name done many wonderful works? And then will I profess unto them, I never knew you: depart from me, ye that work iniquity.
> —Matthew 7:21-23

Inarguably, the Word of God teaches that *many* will follow the road to destruction. Therefore, if *many* will follow this road then should we not think that—since there are *many* different denominations who preach the doctrine of salvation inconsistently with the Word of God—maybe some of these have a chance of being included also, especially when the passage above depicts those claiming to have done great works for God? Today, mainstream Christianity commonly views the modern apostolic church as *prideful & arrogant* for claiming to understand the *only* means of salvation. But even in the four Gospels and the book of Acts we learn that the Pharisees viewed Jesus and the apostles as being arrogant for the same reason. Case in Point: others too often mistake bold confidence for arrogance. Personally, I used to question this myself. However, wouldn't it be more ridiculous if God's true church was *not* confident enough to claim that they have the only way of salvation? The apostles believed that we must . . .

> . . . hold fast the profession of our faith <u>without wavering</u>;
>
> —Hebrews 10:23

"Wavering from the faith" is what caused denominationalism in the first place. Furthermore, what would God think of His church if they did *not* claim to be His true church? To those of you who believe denominationalism is acceptable in the sight of God and that every member of every church will make it to Heaven simply because they go under the "Christian" name: *if the Bible says there is only one true church of God and one true belief system* (Eph 4:4-6), *and if the Bible also speaks against denominationalism* (I Cor 1:10-13), *then why should anyone who claims to be a Christian believe anything contrary?*

As I mentioned in the previous chapter, when distinguishing the one true church of God we should not walk into it as if it were *Multiple-Choice;* we should think more along the lines of *True-or-False.* Consider the fact that Christianity has more sects and divisions than any other belief system in the world? You don't find thousands of denominations in Islam, Buddhism, Hinduism, or any other world religions (though there may be a few with minor differences). The reason is because when it comes to Christianity, the devil, who is *the author of confusion*, does not want people to find the one and only true church of God or understand the only doctrine of salvation in which the apostles preached. His goal is to place Christians in the great sea of denominational churches in order for them to be lost forever and left wondering which church is the true church. Yet it is more commonly suggested that the different denominations are simply *"Worshiping God the way they feel comfortable doing so."*

This whole to-each-his-own attitude has become the most common view of denominationalism these days. People no longer believe the gate to hell is *"wide"* or that *"the path to destruction is broad."* Today's generation suggests quite the opposite. Modern Christianity has turned around these very words of Christ. Nevertheless, the Bible still says there is only *one* body and *one* belief system (Eph 4:4-6) and that there are to be absolutely *no* divisions among Christianity (I Cor 1:10). If we truly believe in the Bible as we claim then we should not just sit back in approval of the various denominations by *"agreeing to disagree."* Because too many people do not want to deal with confrontation they have basically placed their stamp of approval on the various forms of Christianity, whether the doctrines are true or false. But whatever happened to standing up for what we believe in? Have we forgotten our expectations?

> . . . it was needful for me to write unto you, and exhort you <u>that ye should earnestly contend for the faith which was once delivered unto the saints.</u>
>
> —Jude 3

While many do have good intentions through their zealous efforts of upholding their denominational code, we must all get something straight: Standing for Truth is not the same as justifying man-made practice. There is a difference between "contending" for the apostolic faith and quarreling defensively about your own traditions. People can live a *form* of Christianity without actually walking in true Light:

> Ever learning, and never able to come to the knowledge of the truth.
>
> —II Timothy 3:7

Fulfillment at its Best

And they shall turn away their ears from the truth, and shall be turned unto fables.

—II Timothy 4:4

Allow me to share a very unfortunate situation involving the pastor of a secular-nondenominational church (sorry, no names), who questioned some of the things in which I have offered throughout this book. There were a few questions and remarks which he made and were surprising to hear from the mouth of a pastor. Even so, the statements were as follows:

➤ He told me that I *"believe something very dangerous,"* because I believe that following the doctrines of *Repentance, Baptism in Jesus' name,* and the *infilling of the Holy Ghost* are absolute principles which pertain to our salvation—even though this was inarguably what Jesus first delivered to the apostles and is what *they* believed (John 3:5, Mark 16:16, Acts 2:38, see Heb 6:1-2, etc).

➤ He stated that it is *"close-minded to believe that there is only one belief system in which a person can make it to Heaven by"*—even though this is what the apostles believed (I Cor 15:1-3, Eph 4:4-6, Heb 5:9).

➤ He said *"You should not be a part of an organization that believes others will go to hell just because they reject what you preach"*—even though this is what Jesus taught the disciples, and it's what they believed (John 3:5, Mark 16:16, II Thess 1:8-9). Furthermore, true apostles only relay what the Bible says. We do not place judgment upon or make determinations for any individual (Rom 10:6). Judgment is up to God alone.

➤ He asked, *"How can you believe that there is only one church organization that is correct in its beliefs?"* Well, because the Bible says so; this is what the apostles preached (I Cor 1:10, Eph 4:4-6).

➢ He stated that he *"does not agree with Catholicism,"* but that he is *"not going to say their belief is wrong"*—even though the Bible teaches us to contend for the faith (Jude 3) and to tell people when they are mistaken in their beliefs (II Tim 4:2).

➢ After assuring me that he would *"die believing in the trinity"* he stated that he does *"not care about the origin of the trinity doctrine or who first thought of it."* Afterward he tried to convince me that, *"We shouldn't question things about God just because we don't understand them."*

Does this mean we should not question why we are following man-made doctrines instead of the apostles' doctrine? The whole reason this book came into existence is because I questioned my own faith. And as a result, through immense studying (II Tim 2:15) and historical archive digging (Rom 15:4) I uncovered exactly where and why so many forms of Christianity entered the world and which doctrines are extra-biblical. As a former Trinitarian, now converted and buried with Christ through baptism, filled with His one-and-only Spirit and unshakably founded in the Oneness-Pentecostal doctrine of the Apostolic Faith, I must reiterate this: It is our responsibility—and God's expectation for us—to do our research, correctly explain the Bible (II Tim 2:15), and to have a knowledge of the past (Rom 15:4) in order to know beyond a shadow of a doubt that we are walking in absolute Truth rather than simply accepting and following the traditions in which we are familiar (comfortable) with! And no matter what we may have been raised to believe or whatever we currently view as the truth, one thing is absolute: *God our Savior will have all men come unto the knowledge of the Truth* (I Tim 2:3-4).

Now, let's reflect on the most disturbing comment in which this pastor imparted:

"You should not be a part of an organization that believes others will go to hell just because they reject what you preach."

How hypocritical is that? I assumed that being the pastor of a church he would be a little more zealous for that which he preaches. But then again, if you really don't believe that what you are preaching is the "only way" then there is really no place for zeal. Make sense? Not that we should wish anyone to hell, but we should at least believe that what we are preaching is the only true way of salvation. Unfortunately, as it is in the case of this so-called pastor, instead of *"contending for the faith"* (Jude 3) it is more common to see others justify their preferred *form* of godliness. More to the point: if a person (pastors especially) does not truly believe that what he is preaching is the *only* way to be saved then what business does he have preaching it and where does his faith truly lie? And just to elaborate further on the statement above; saying this only *proves* whether a person truly understands absolute doctrine—that or it exemplifies whether or not a person truly believes in what he preaches. I mean, if you *do* understand Truth or truly believe in what you preach then how much sense does it make to sit back and approve of the many "Christian" divisions throughout the globe who preach diverse doctrines and cannot agree. Make sense?

How this pertains to both you and I: ultimately, whether you are a part of a secular denomination or the only body of Christ, if you *don't* believe that your denominational code (or belief) is the *only* way a person can be saved then what good will it do anyone for you to share your faith, especially if people have alternative options? How can your outreach efforts benefit others when you believe they can follow various paths and still make it to Heaven? Ask yourself: *Do you believe that your current denominational code is the only way a person can be saved; or do you believe that any organization under the "Christian" name is good enough?*

The danger of teachers who do not fully grasp the apostles' doctrine is that they do not understand the seriousness of issues pertaining to salvation; therefore, they often dismiss certain models or denote certain commands as "optional" in receiving salvation (commands such as baptism, etc). In essence, these types describe *"blind guides leading the blind"* (Matt 15:14). The fact is that teaching the "option" of obedience to certain commands only works against others in that, if one believes he can still be saved even by neglecting a few particular commands then he may contemplate further what more he can get away with and still be a Christian. Basically, the mindset is: *"If I can get away with 'this' then I can get away with 'that'!"* Moreover, the danger of teachers that do not understand the seriousness of commands pertaining to salvation is this:

> *Whosoever therefore shall break one of these least commandments, <u>and shall teach men so</u>, he shall be called the least in the kingdom of heaven:*
> —Matthew 5:19

To further set things into perspective let's visit the event of Peter's forbiddance to the Lord as He enlightened the disciples of His soon-coming crucifixion:

> From that time forth began Jesus to shew unto his disciples, how that he must go unto Jerusalem, and suffer many things . . . and be killed . . . Then Peter took him, and began to rebuke him, saying, Be it far from thee, Lord: this shall not be unto thee. But he turned and said unto Peter, *Get thee behind me, Satan; for thou savourest not the things that be of God, but those that be of men.*
> —Matthew 16:21-23

Obviously, Peter had difficulty accepting the truth—even to the point that he attempted to prevent the will of God—and in turn the Lord rebuked him for it. Likewise, when we resist the will of God or try to prevent others from receiving His plan of salvation—no matter who we are, what we already know, how close to God we *think* we may be or even if we believe we *are* in God's will—then . . . well, I will just let the passage above speak for itself (notice Jesus' response). Men and brethren, if we are not willing to forsake everything—including our *opinions* or what we *assume* is biblically accurate—then frankly, we cannot be the Lord's disciple:

> *So likewise, whosoever he be of you that forsaketh not all*
> *that he hath, he cannot be my disciple.*
> —Luke 14:33

In case you didn't know there is compromise involved in actually living for God as opposed to merely attending church services regularly. As I stated in the introduction, I do not doubt that anyone, who may be a part of any denomination, nondenominational, or Catholic organization can have a relationship with God. God can reach anyone-anywhere. I know many people who love God and are serving Him to the best of their knowledge and ability. Yet everyone must understand that we can't just settle for the *form* of Christianity we are most comfortable with or that we may have been raised in.

"I'm Not Gonna Budge!"

I cannot even begin to recall how many times I have heard—or heard of—strong believers who have stated, *"There's got to be something deeper to the Gospel; something I haven't seen before."* Many seem to be aware that there is more depth to the Gospel than what appears on the surface; more than what is offered in the usual denominational Sunday morning sermons. Yet when these same people are faced with the original doctrines of the apostles (*Jesus-name baptism, the Oneness view of the Godhead, or the infilling of the Holy Ghost*) they remain biased because of the convenience of their current tradition, whereas it is familiar and comfortable to them. A very tragic reality is that there will be more who hear and reject the Truth than will accept it. Even throughout the Bible we see souls who were *almost* persuaded of the Gospel-Truth:

> Then Agrippa said unto Paul, Almost thou persuadest
> me to be a Christian.
>
> —Acts 26:28

Too many reject the Truth after counting the cost (Mark 10:17-22). Some, who, once they have been enlightened of Truth—like many people today—simply cannot accept *that* which they hear:

> Many therefore of his disciples, when they had heard
> this, said, This is an hard saying; who can hear it? . . .
> From that time many of his disciples walked no more
> with him.
>
> —John 6:60, 66

Basically, many will reject Truth because it isn't what they are expecting or hoping for. In other words, it doesn't tickle their ears. Tragically, if a person rejects the only doctrine of Truth when it is offered to them then they may continue to search for something they previously rejected. If we cannot accept the basic principles of Christianity as being pertinent in receiving salvation then we are spiritually limited:

> *If any man have ears to hear, let him hear . . . . Take*
> *head what ye hear: <u>with what measure ye mete, it shall</u>*
> *<u>be measured to you: and unto you that hear shall more be</u>*
> *<u>given</u>.*
>
> —Mark 4:23-24

In essence, we should not expect "more" to be given unto us if we do not accept that which was initially offered on the Day of Pentecost; the very steps which begin our new birth as a Christian. If we do not accept the doctrine of salvation presented by the apostles (or the doctrine of the Oneness of God) then we are spiritually limited to receive much of what we are capable of. We cannot progress until we have a definite understanding of the fundamentals. Hebrews 6:1-2 teaches us to leave the elementary teachings of Christ in order to mature into the perfected saint we were meant to be. Therefore, we must first understand that we cannot *leave* the fundamentals and move on if we have already *skipped* them in the first place. Now, this does not mean some are incapable of learning *anything* more just because they have never been exposed to the Truth; it just means that Satan knows what sets boundaries in the spiritual maturing process and what can prevent us from reaching our full potential. Moreover, we must humbly accept that which was initially offered the day the New Covenant was bound in Heaven in order to grow.

Still, there are more reasons *why* some will never come to accept absolute doctrine. Sometimes the comfort of current acquaintances—depending on the level of one's involvement in the church—may play a huge part in why a person will never respond to the sound doctrine in which another church may offer. They cannot find it in themselves to leave a church which they have been a part of for so long; they won't allow themselves to disconnect from the social connection in which their current church organization offers, thusly remaining in a paralyzed state of spiritual complacency simply because they will not respond to that which God is revealing to them. Nevertheless, we must remember that Jesus' *requirement* for us is to be willing to compromise any human relationship for Him (Matt 10:34-37). (As for those who are *not* held back by the social connection in their church the tendency is to search in other areas—even church-swapping to denominations further away from the Truth (probably because of less conviction).)

And then there are those who cannot accept absolute doctrine because it involves submission to authority. More specifically and just to be blunt, there is a difference between being what society views as *"Christian"* and being an actual *"holy and separated saint of God."* (I know I'm speaking to somebody.) When viewing the churches today who preach accordingly to the apostles' doctrine of salvation we find that most practice *separation*, while certain denominationalists more or less promote what I like to call *Secular-Christianity*. More specifically, the secular-Christian mindset today is that you can watch and listen to whatever you want, dress however you please, go wherever places you want, affiliate yourself with whoever, and say whatever comes to mind (not only in the slang words but also in topic of conversation), while still being a "Christian."

Even though the early church we read about in Scripture was under submission to very specific standards the mindset today is that we can disregard whichever models or customs that do not appeal to us. Basically, too many "Christians" do not want to be separate from the world; they do not want *holiness*. Therefore, many will miss the mark simply because being separate from the world is not appealing. I would even dare to say that we've tried to blend as much Hollywood in with our so-called "Christian" lives that we no longer know what it even means to be separate from the world. Unfortunately and consequently, many Christians have already been duped into believing they *are* separate from the world when actually they are not.

The truth is that while there is a church who understands principles such as *submission* and *separation from the world* there will always be gainsayers who speak against that which they do not understand simply because they do not want to submit to anything further (Jude 10). Too many modern church members are more focused on how they can blend worldly lifestyles with their Christian walk while they should be asking God what more they can eliminate to be closer to Him. Not only does God love it when people do extra for him but He also Loves It when people do extra for Him! (Need I say it again?) And the tragic irony involved with mere *forms* of godliness is that many who live these effortless lifestyles claim to believe in the same Bible that speaks against the lifestyle they currently live. But here is where the rubber meets the road:

> For I bear them record that they have a zeal of God, but not according to knowledge. Far they being ignorant of God's righteousness, and going about to establish their own righteousness, have not submitted themselves unto the righteousness of God.
>
> —Romans 10:2-3

Overall, it is typical for a person who has been shown the Truth, for him to deny or later turn his back on it (backsliding) after seeing what all it involves or what is expected of them (I was one of these). And because too many want to be *"saved by grace"* and nothing more they tent to move backward in their spiritual journey simply because of denial (even denying historical proof which disproves his or her tradition). Yet we must be humble enough to admit that it's not about what WE want or what is convenient for US! If "Truth" is only a matter of opinion—if it is acceptable in the sight of God to interpret the Gospel any way we want—then apparently the apostles were overly-up-tight about warning the churches of such detrimental philosophies and theologies entering the church.

Ultimately, if a person cannot accept the truths in which we have covered, which are boldly written in black and white, then he or she will remain living a mere "form of godliness" (II Tim 3:5), thusly limiting themselves from anything further (Mark 4:24). Nevertheless, these truths will never go away. These things are not only written in the Bible but are confirmed in secular history as well. What we have covered will remain and will continue to grow until the coming of the Lord. It's never been about spreading *forms* of Christianity around the globe; it's about spreading the *only* Gospel-Truth to all nations!

> *And this gospel of the kingdom shall be preached in all the world for a witness unto all nations; and then shall the end come.*
> —Matthew 24:14

The Acts 19 Reality

The best way I can think of to identify with mainstream Christianity today is to revisit Acts chapter 19 again and again. If you recall, the Apostle Paul met up with some fellow believers; John's disciples; people who were already Christians. As we have already established these people already had a relationship with Jesus Christ, yet that did not change the fact that they still had to be born of the water and Spirit in order to fulfill the salvation plan in which Jesus first spoke of in John 3:5.

The following is a short conversation I had with my sister-in-law, who once *was* one of these people depicted in Acts chapter 19. Just like me, her spiritual eyes began to see the deeper truths of the Gospel after *humbly* accepting what the Bible clearly states rather than *simply* accepting the man-made traditions in which she was accustomed to. Even so, the conversation (via text message) went as follows:

Sister-in-law: I really feel like the Oneness of the Godhead is a major milestone in helping others understand the truth about salvation. I mean, you gotta know WHO God is before you can understand His escape plan.

Me: Bingo! What sets the one true church of God apart from all other organizations is: knowing the true identity of God and understanding what the apostles taught on the subject of salvation. The kicker is that these doctrines (Oneness and baptism) are so intertwined with each other.

Sister-in-law: That's so true!

Me: Something difficult to accept is that if we are truly hungry for God like we claim then we should be doing our part and seeking Truth at all costs instead of ignoring what we don't want to accept. People don't like to hear the truth because our itching ears tend to look for easier ways to make it to Heaven.

Sister-in-law: Right! People just want to believe "God accepts everyone just the way we are" and that nothing is required from us. It seems like that's where the bus stops with secular denominations. They think you don't have to be "transformed" (Rom 12:2) to be a Christian as long as you attend their church and are a "good person."

> **Me:** That's why I love Acts ch. 19 so much! It talks about people that were "already Christians." But even though they were already followers of Christ it did not change the fact that they still needed to be re-baptized in Jesus' name and filled with the Holy Ghost in order to fulfill the born-again plan!

Sister-in-law: Exactly! It was the same situation with Cornelius too! He was a devout, godly man, but he still needed to go through the "born-again" procedure.

A very tragic reality is that the majority of people who claim to be Christians don't realize how real and alive the Word of God is (Heb 4:12) or how much he or she is involved with prophecy. Everyone exists in a world that revolves around the Bible, and everything that is written applies to both you and me. Since we know that the Bible says there is only ONE body, ONE belief system, and ONE way to be saved (Eph 4:4-5), we must understand that God—who can reach anyone-anywhere—has given us our entire lives to find out who, what, and where this one and only body of believers is and how to become a part of it. We must devote our lives to seeking Truth, which means that we must *compare* the different church doctrines to the Bible and live up to our expectations in studying history in order that we may know and have full assurance that we are walking in the Light! Moreover, if we considered our present spiritual state as being *sufficient* in gaining salvation, whether we have accepted the apostles' doctrine or not, there would be no cause to search any further for God.

It seems as though the majority of claimed Christians assume that because they are a part of an organization that is "Christ-centered," they are already "saved." However, the Bible lets us know that no matter who we are or what we already know (Acts 10:34), God—though firm in keeping every promise—is being patient with us so that we will not be lost (II Peter 3:9). His desire is for ALL people to come to the knowledge of Truth (I Tim 2:3-4). What classifies the true church and body of Christ is NOT the name or denomination of the organization; it's all about being of one mind in knowing who God is and understanding the apostle's doctrine of salvation.

Tragically, what itching ears don't want to hear is what was first spoken by the Lord (Mark 16:16, Luke 24:47, John 3:5) and confirmed by the words and actions of the apostles (Acts 2:38; 19:1-6). Itching ears don't want to hear that they need to carry out the Great Commission the same way as the apostles instead of following the tradition of men. Itching ears don't want to hear that—even though they firmly believe the Pentecostal experience was a part of the early church—it is still a promise available unto ALL (Acts 2:39). Itching ears don't want to hear that the very same ordinances and customs which were true for the early church are to be applied to today also. Itching ears don't want to hear that the Trinitarian model of the Godhead (the three-in-one tripartite) is an extra-biblical theology which we were warned of (Col 2:8-10). Moreover, itching ears want only a *form* of Christianity and not what the apostles initially offered. Itching ears want tradition, not Truth:

> Having a form of godliness, but denying the power thereof: . . . Ever learning, and never able to come to the knowledge of the truth.
>
> —II Timothy 3:5, 7

Instead of conforming to true Christianity *entirely* the majority of us would rather add only a limited amount of God to OUR OWN lifestyle. Because too many souls are focused on the here-and-now they only want an *image* of Christianity—having one foot in the church—while rejecting the very principles in which Christianity was founded upon (having the other foot in the world). Too many want to be known as a Christian yet will not accept everything in which the Lord offers.

❖ The Network:

> And in that day seven women shall take hold of one man, saying, We will eat our own bread, and wear our

own apparel: only let us be called by thy name, to take
away our reproach.

—Isaiah 4:1

As I stated in Chapter One, my intention is *not* to bring
division among a particular church body; it is to distinguish the
willing from the unwilling. If you have access to your local library
or internet then I encourage you to search some of the topics this
book covers, whereas these topics are the core of what sets the true
church of God apart from Catholicism, Trinitarianism, and secular
denominationalism. However, these are only the highlights. The
people I've mentioned, along with their alterations to the Gospel,
are the very instruments Satan used to blind the eyes of the elect.
Unfortunately we cannot escape the deceptive clutches of the
enemy if we continue to feed our itching ears with messages that
don't convict us or if we continue to *ignore* that which was first
spoken by the Lord and confirmed by the words and actions of
the apostles. Remember, the Bible even asks:

How shall we escape, if we neglect so great salvation;
which at the first began to be spoken by the Lord, and
was confirmed unto us by them that heard him;

—Hebrews 2:3

What it all boils down to is what you will do with what has
been revealed to you (James 1:22). Whether you *have* or *have not*
heard these teachings prior to reading this book, the fact is that
you now know. Your Bible still contains the things in which I have
attempted to unveil. Even though many will continue to revert
back to Romans 10:9 to justify why nothing beyond *believing* in
Jesus is required to attain salvation, frankly, nothing will ever emit
what is written in John 3:5, Mark 16:16, Luke 24:47, Acts 2:38,
etc. The fact is that the way of righteousness has been revealed to
you; therefore, I urge you not to turn from it. Eternity is too long,
and hell is too miserable to ignore this way of righteousness:

> For it had been better for them not to have known the
> way of righteousness, than, after they have known it,
> to turn from the holy commandment delivered unto
> them.
>
> —II Peter 2:21

Even though many will continue to cling to the notion that *"God knows the heart, and that's all that matters"* while denying the very principles in which we have discussed, the fact is this: whether or not one is able to accept and apply some of these topics may essentially *determine* the condition of his heart. Remember, in the introduction I asked three challenging questions: *How humble are you* (Psalm 69:32); *How hungry are you* (Jeremiah 29:13); *Are you "testing the spirits"* (I John 4:1)? Now, even though it may take some time for these things to sink in, I would ask that you spend the near future contemplating what you have read.

> Therefore, we ought to give the more earnest heed to
> the things which we have heard, lest at any time we
> should let them slip.
>
> —Hebrews 2:1

Consider the Pharisees one last time. Though these men were affiliated with what God had established nearly fourteen-hundred years prior, He was discontented in what they had made of His covenants. Additionally, they were blind to the fact that God was displeased with the traditionalism which took place of His commands (Mark 7:9, 13). Likewise, even though Christianity was first presented to the world with very specific standards, customs, guidelines and only one plan of salvation by monotheistic apostles, it is what the Catholic Church and the denominational establishments have made of Christianity that must be observed.

Like the Pharisees, many denominationalists will never come to grips with this reality as history repeats itself once again. Yet if every Christian truly stopped to think about the Great Day of Judgment and the accounts which we are expected to give then how many of us would be able to defend the Catholic traditions we chose to follow over the original doctrines of the apostles? How many of us would be able to justify our preferred form of godliness (II Tim 3:5)—especially since we have the capability of becoming a born-again child of God through the *only* salvation plan bound in Heaven?

Notice the following passage one last time. Remember, this is not describing lost sinners. It is evident that Jesus is referring to people that were Christians during their earthly lives; believers that were living for God, doing mighty works for Him. Yet they were turned away from His glorious presence:

> *Many will say to me in that day, Lord, Lord, have we not prophesied in thy name? and in thy name have cast out devils? and in thy name done many wonderful works? And then will I profess unto them, I never knew you: depart from me, ye that work iniquity.*
> —Matthew 7:22-23

As the passage above affirms, many, who don't understand what it means to fear the Lord, assuming their efforts were *"good enough,"* believing they are *"already saved"* because they have been *"going to church for years"* . . . will miss the mark, simply because they've rejected the salvation plan which is bound in Heaven. Moreover, What Itching Ears Don't Want to Hear is the most relevant words of Christ which pertain to the pharisaic, denominational traditionalists of today as history repeats itself once again . . .

❖ The Network ❖

> *. . . Howbeit in vain do they worship me, teaching for doctrines the commandments of men. For laying aside the commandment of God, ye hold the tradition of men, . . . Full well ye reject the commandment of God, that ye may keep your own tradition. Making the word of God of none effect through your tradition, which ye have delivered:*
> —Mark 7:7-9, 13

Matthew 28:19 ... Forged?

For there is nothing covered, that shall not be revealed; neither hid, that shall not be known.

—Luke 12:2

The Catholic Encyclopedia, II, pg 263 summarizes the following: The baptismal formula was changed from the name of Jesus Christ to the phrase "Father, Son, Holy Spirit" by the Catholic Church in the second century. On this page the Catholic Church acknowledges and agrees that baptism was originally performed in the name of the Lord Jesus Christ by the early church (and even references the book of Acts) but was simulated throughout time. Additionally, this page offers various formulas that were practiced by certain sects throughout time, though only one prevailed among mainstream Christianity (repeating Matthew 28:19). Thus, merely quoting a simple phrase is what replaced the original method of the apostles' baptism that was confirmed on the Day of Pentecost and bound in Heaven.

Catholic Cardinal Joseph Ratzinger: *"The basic form of our* (Matthew 28:19 Trinitarian) *profession of faith took shape during the course of the second and third centuries in connection with the ceremony of baptism. So far as its place of origin is concerned, the text of Matthew 28:19 therefore did not originate from the original Church that started in Jerusalem around AD 33. It was rather as the evidence proves a later invention of Roman Catholicism completely fabricated. Very few know about these historical facts."*

"The Demonstratio Evangelica" by Eusebius quotes Matthew 28:19 as he sees the original manuscripts it in its unaltered form in the Library of Caesarea. His testimony: *"With one word and voice He said to His disciples: "Go, and make disciples of all nations in My name, teaching them to observe all things whatsoever I have commanded you."*

The Schaff-Herzog Encyclopedia of Religious Knowledge: *"Jesus, however, cannot have given His disciples this Trinitarian order of baptism after His resurrection; for the New Testament knows only* *one baptism in the name of Jesus* (Acts 2:38; 8:16; 10:43; 19:5; Gal. 3:27; Rom. 6:3; I Cor. 1:13-15), *which still occurs even in the second and third centuries, while the Trinitarian formula occurs only in Matt. 28:19, and then only again* (in the) *Didache 7:1 and Justin, Apol. 1:61 . . . Finally, the distinctly liturgical character of the formula . . . is strange; it was not the way of Jesus to make such formulas . . . the formal authenticity of Matt. 28:19 must be disputed . . ."* page 435.

The Jerusalem Bible, a scholarly Catholic work, states: *"It may be that this formula,* (Triune Matthew 28:19) *so far as the fullness of its expression is concerned, is a reflection of the* (Man-made) *liturgical usage established later in the primitive* (Catholic) *community. It will be remembered that Acts speaks of baptizing "in the name of Jesus,"*

The International Standard Bible Encyclopedia, Vol. 4, pg 2637, under "Baptism,": *"Matthew 28:19 in particular only canonizes a later ecclesiastical situation, that its universalism is contrary to the facts of early Christian history, and its Trinitarian formula* (is) *foreign to the mouth of Jesus."*

New Revised Standard Version says this about Matthew 28:19: *"Modern critics claim this formula is falsely ascribed to Jesus and that it represents later* (Catholic) *church tradition, for nowhere in the book of Acts* (or any other book of the Bible) *is baptism performed with the name of the Trinity . . ."*

The Bible Commentary 1919 pg 723: *"The command to baptize into the threefold name is a late doctrinal expansion. Instead of the words baptizing them in the name of the Father, and of the Son, and of the Holy Ghost we should probably read simply—"into My Name."*

A great reference to confirm the accuracy of the apostles' baptism method can be found at **www.upcbaypoint.com/Articles2/early_church_baptism. html**

This site offers a unique perspective and further insight of the Truth as well as many more supportive encyclopedic references. Permission to use this website as a reference was granted by Pastor Donald O'keefe of the United Pentecostal Church of Bay Point, California.

Author's Note

If you are reading this now—whether you consider yourself to be just another "Ordinary Joe" or if you happen to be the editor himself—then I commend you for enduring throughout this entire journey and accepting such a challenging endeavor. I also hope that my *confidence* in everything I've offered will not be mistaken as *arrogance*. Whether or not this book makes a difference in the world can only be determined by individual response. I truly hope and pray that these *pearls* in which I have to offer will not end up in the hands of unappreciative *swine* (Matthew 7:6). Furthermore, I would like to thank each and every minister of the apostolic faith who has helped instill these principles in my spirit (many of you probably don't even know I'm referring to you). That being said—and because we all have a Heaven to gain and a hell to shun—I bid you all Godspeed in your search for Truth!